Danann
BOOKS

GRAND PRIX

A HISTORY THROUGH THE LENS

Danann
BOOKS

First Published Danann Publishing Ltd 2016

WARNING: For private domestic use only, any unauthorised Copying, hiring,
lending or public performance of this book is illegal.

Photography courtesy of:
GETTY IMAGES;

Hulton Archive / Stringer	**Rolls Press/Popperfoto /**	**Anton Want / Staff**
Heritage Images / Contributor	**Contributor**	**Tobias Heyer / Staff**
Dennis Oulds / Stringer	**Paul Popper/Popperfoto /**	**Patrick Hertzog / Staff**
Popperfoto / Contributor	**Contributor**	**Damien Meyer / Staff**
Gp Library / Contributor	**Mondadori Portfolio /**	**Paul Gilham / Staff**
Howard Sochurek /	**Contributor**	**Robert Cianflone / Staff**
Contributor	**Grand Prix Photo /**	**Mark Thompson / Staff**
Klemantaski Collection /	**Contributor**	**Clive Mason / Staff**
Contributor	**Tony Feder / Stringer**	**Prakash Singh / Staff**
Rainer W. Schlegelmilch /	**Pascal Rondeau / Staff**	**Dimitar Dilkoff / Staff**
Contributor	**Simon Bruty / Staff**	
Central Press / Stringer	**Michael Kunkel / Staff**	

All other images Wiki Commons

Book layout & design Darren Grice at Ctrl-d

Made in EU.
CAT NO: DAN0293
ISBN: 978-0-9930169-7-4

CONTENTS

HOW IT ALL BEGAN

They invented the wheel, so why the ancient Mesopotamians weren't hurtling around racetracks 3,500 years ago is beyond the understanding of anyone who loves motor racing. The world had to wait for the Mycenaean Greeks to turn up, it seems, (thankfully they did) before spectators could enjoy the thrill of wheeled speed racing; pottery fragments appear to confirm that these fearless pioneers were charging around in chariots sometime around 1600—1100 BC. What on earth did the ancients do with their Sunday afternoons before that?

And another thing; why did it then take until 1886 to produce the first motorcar?

Fine, we won't go into that, but thank you Herr Karl Benz for his Benz Patent-Motorwagen; thankfully he — and his wife Bertha — turned up, too. From then on it was all, well, not downhill, exactly, more... round and round in distorted circles.

Anyway. Back to that sepia past.

It's the year 1894. Herr Benz's motorcar has now been joined by many others, and no country is more enthusiastic for this new method of fast travel than France. Car manufacturers well understood the value of a competition that would show off their shiny new vehicles, and on the 22 July that year, Le Petit Journal, a Paris newspaper, organised the first 'official' race in the history of the Grand Prix. That first race also brought motor racing's first scandal. Zut alors! Well, a disqualification, in fact. The racetrack stretched for over 70 miles (126 kilometres) between Porte Maillot in Paris and Rouen. Having completed the course in six hours forty-eight minutes at an average, and mind-boggling, speed of 12 miles an hour (19.3 km/h), first over the line in Rouen was Count Jules-Albert de Dion. However, the count's car was steam driven and it needed a stoker to keep it fuelled. On account of this, the judges, who were looking for safety, controllability and economy, disqualified the Count and ruled that second-placed Albert Lemaître, driving a Peugeot Type 7, 3hp, with his co-driver/mechanic Adolf

Clemént-Bayard, a bicycle manufacturer, had taken first place. (There were joint winners, Auguste Doriot, René Panhard and Émile Levassor, as the cars were not judged on speed alone.) Albert had arrived at the finish line 3½ minutes behind de Dion.

(In fact, there was another, real scandal involving Albert, because in 1906, after his wife had filed for divorce, the two of them began an argument and Albert shot and killed her, before turning the gun on himself. The bullet to his head failed to kill him, however, and he was acquitted of a crime of passion.)

Nonetheless, motor racing was here to stay, and over the following years, motor races became a firm event in many French towns. Émile Levassor was evidently still a car enthusiast a year later, because in 1895 he won the race that year again, even though he was refused the FR. 31,000 prize because his car only had two seats instead of four. His drive was an extraordinary feat of endurance; he had hardly stopped during the 48 hours 48 minutes of his race. This 1895 event was notable for the fact that a certain André Michelin had entered the race in a car boasting pneumatic tyres. This newfangled invention must have caused a good few raised eyebrows amongst aficionados, because poor André suffered many humiliating punctures along the route. So they would obviously never catch on.

1895 was also the year that saw the formation of the Automobile Club de France (ACF), and the first race event ever held in Italy. Those thrilling and startling speeds of 9.6mph were achieved over a 57-mile (93km) course, but in the years to the end of the century, the search for increased speed gathered pace and 7 and 8-litre engines began to make their appearance.

It was an American, James Gordon Bennett, who wrote the next chapter in the history of motor racing. His father was the founder, editor and publisher of the New York Herald. Gordon junior was a sports enthusiast, who had been educated largely in France, and in 1866 he took over the New York Herald from his father. Gordon did not drive, yet in 1899, with a newspaperman's eye for publicity, he organised what came to be known as the Gordon Bennett Cup Race, six international races held annually between 1900 and 1906. France,

Germany, Great Britain, Italy, the United States, Belgium, Switzerland, and Austria all competed. The cars had to have two side-by-side seats occupied by the driver and a mechanic. The first race — the average speed by now was a hair-raising 38.6 mph (62.1km/h) — was won by Fernand Charron driving a Panhard-Levassor (yes, you guessed correctly, the very same Monsieur Émile Levassor; although, sadly, he had died in 1897 following an automobile accident the previous year).

International colours were assigned to the competitors for the first time; blue for France, white for Germany, red to the USA, yellow for Belgium, with Britain (which first competed in 1902) choosing green and Italy only adopting its 'racing red' in 1907. Ireland hosted the race at Athy in 1903, and this was the first ever, closed-circuit race to take place, even though it was run over public roads.

But we're getting ahead of ourselves, slightly.

It was in 1901 that motor sport accelerated out of its infancy with the introduction of the 35hp Mercedes and a four-cylinder engine with mechanical valves and... zut alors, encore...! those hopeless pneumatic tyres, which were, of course, no longer hopeless. Having reached 35hp, however, the mechanics didn't stay there long, and the engine capacity of the Mercedes rapidly increased to 9 litres producing 60hp. The speeds rocketed accordingly; in the 1901 Gordon Bennett Cup race, the open Mors of Fournier reached an average speed of 53 mph (85.2 km/h).

That year is considered to be the birthday of the Grand Prix; the race that took place at Le Mans was the first to be described as a Grand Prix, and it was the Hungarian Ferencz Szisz driving a Renault, which boasted a 90hp engine, who raced into the history books by finishing first. He had covered the 700-mile course at an average of 63 mph (101km/h).

Meanwhile, the Gordon Bennett Cup race was still going strong, and in 1903 in spectacular style, Camille Jenatzy created a sensation by driving with his foot down to the floor in a spine-tingling race that brought him the winner's cup and £8,000. Even more spectacular that year was the Paris-Bordeaux race; these were described as ***"fearsome, thrilling fights"***, but they claimed the lives of drivers and spectators alike, and in 1903, the French authorities called it a day. They stopped the race and confiscated the cars; it proved to

Karl Benz

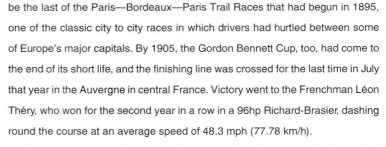

be the last of the Paris—Bordeaux—Paris Trail Races that had begun in 1895, one of the classic city to city races in which drivers had hurtled between some of Europe's major capitals. By 1905, the Gordon Bennett Cup, too, had come to the end of its short life, and the finishing line was crossed for the last time in July that year in the Auvergne in central France. Victory went to the Frenchman Léon Théry, who won for the second year in a row in a 96hp Richard-Brasier, dashing round the course at an average speed of 48.3 mph (77.78 km/h).

That victory seemed to prove what every Frenchman already knew, that France was the leading motor racing country, and the French automobile industry, the largest in Europe, now wanted a competition to reflect this status. So, the AFC organised the Grand Prix for manufacturers on the 26 and 27 June 1906. But because so many drivers and spectators had already died during the sport's brief years of existence, organisers changed their ideas. This race would take place on a closed circuit, outside the city of Le Mans, along a route of 64.11 miles (103.18 kilometres). Each competitor would complete six laps over two days.

The race took place in heat so fierce it melted the tar of the roads, which was kicked up into the driver's faces, and those pneumatic tyres — there were some who still said *"I told you so"* — were continually getting punctures, although defective radiators and wheels were the biggest culprits in cars that failed to complete the course. There was a well-known face in the winning Renault car, Ferenc Szisz, with Felice Nazzaro coming in second and another driver who was also well known by this time, Clément-Bayard, taking third place.

The race, ever afterwards to be known as the first Grand Prix, was not considered to have been as exciting as the Gordon Bennett Cup races, but, nonetheless, it was organised again in 1907 and inspired Germany to organise its own race that year, the Kaiserpreis, The Kaiser's Prize, which eventually became the German Grand Prix. 1907 was also the year in which the almost oval-shaped, steep banks of the Brooklands racetrack in England were completed.

So, the Grand Prix had firmly imprinted itself in the sporting calendar of Europe after just a decade on the roads. After a conference in 1904 it even had its own governing body, which had debated a French proposal for a change in format to the Gordon Bennett races; many national clubs then joined forces to found the Association Internationale des Automobile Clubs Reconnus, the AIACR, which later became the Fédération Internationale de l'Automobile, the regulating body for international motor sport.

Christian Lautenschlager

In this exciting new age of motor racing, France lost its dominance and yielded space to the upstarts Alfa of Italy and especially Mercedes of Germany. From now on, spectators would be treated to a conveyor belt of new innovations and ever-faster cars. In 1908, shallow emplacements along the side of the track were introduced; the pit had made its appearance and was to be the scene of many a drama in the unfolding spectacle of the sport. The wheel, too, was undergoing a transformation. Although the pneumatic tyre had triumphed and replaced the old solid rubber one and a removable rim had facilitated faster removal of the wheel, the situation was far from satisfactory. In 1908, the Mercedes pit crew's work was made easier when they were given pneumatic jacks, and the cars were fitted with one-bolt wheels, a race-changing, revolutionary development; especially in those early years when tyres would be shredded by the poor road surfaces. Mercedes driver Christian Lautenschlager wrecked ten tyres before he raced over the line victorious that year.

The fierce nationalism involved in the races, let alone the commercial considerations, even at this early stage in the sport — winning manufacturers could expect a surge in sales from financing a winning team — and political wrangling, managed to prevent the Grand Prix from taking place between the years of 1909 and 1911. In the light of what was to come, this inability to allow even a motor race to overcome national pride was a bad omen. So the action moved to America, where the Indianapolis Motor Speedway was first used in 1909, and in 1911 there was another first; the Indianapolis 500-mile Race. Perhaps this galvanised the Grand Prix organisers into working together again, because in 1912, the Grand Prix was back up and running.

Peugeot had been busy refining their cars during the hiatus, and the results paid off immediately. These mighty cars are considered by many to have been the forerunners of the racing cars we know today, because thanks to engineer Ernest Henry, described as *"… perhaps the most brilliant engine designer ever"*, a revolution in racing car technology had taken place; the latest Peugeot engines featured overhead valves inclined in the cylinder heads and operated by two overhead camshafts. It changed the world of racing from then on, and on June 25 and 26 1912, Georges Boillot won the Grand Prix in his Peugeot, after Fiat driver David Bruce-Brown had been disqualified for fuelling his car outside the pits. It was in this race that mechanic Jean Bassignano was killed when the wheel came off his and driver Léon Collinet's car in lap three and the car turned over.

The following year, with five fatalities before the race even started, Georges Boillot and Peugeot were triumphant once again, at Amiens, this time, averaging a speed of 72.141 mph (116.096 km/h). For that 1913 race, the Grand Prix cars had been restricted to a minimum weight of 1,764 lb (800 kg) and a maximum weight of 2,425 lb (1,100 kg), plus a fuel consumption limit of 14 mpg (20 l/100 km).

The Germans, however, had not been sitting 'idling' by as Peugeot went from strength to strength; far from it. They were back with a vengeance for the 1914 Grand Prix and lined up at the start at Lille on 4 July that year. Archduke Franz Ferdinand of Austria and his wife had been assassinated only a few days earlier on the 28 June and tension in Europe, especially between the French and Germans, was palpable.

This Grand Prix is regarded as being one of the greatest events in motor-racing history. Thirteen manufacturers from six different countries entered thirty-seven cars, and for the first time, a limit was set on the size of the engine allowed; 4.5 litres. A new feature of this race was that drivers were controlled by signals from the pit.

Eerily, the Grand Prix became a competition between the French Peugeot and the German Mercedes cars. The Germans dominated the race, despite Boillot taking the lead for twelve of the twenty laps, and the excitement of the 300,000 crowd of spectators was intense. By the time the French driver dropped out on the last lap, Ferenc Szisz, winner of the first Grand Prix, had been hit by a car whilst changing a wheel and broken his arm. The Mercedes cars passed the line in first, second and third places, with Christian Lautenschlager taking the winner's prize. The French onlookers were not pleased.

As the crowd dispersed and the excitement of the Grand Prix faded, there were more serious matters to think about, for within just a few weeks, Europe would be at war. Many of the drivers, the crews, and those admiring of their talents, would not return from the mighty conflict that claimed millions of lives. Amongst them was the driver Georges Boillot. He became a driver for the French Commander-in-Chief, General Joseph Joffre, before joining a flying unit and becoming an ace pilot. He won the Croix de Guerre and the Legion d'Honneur. On April the 21st 1916, engaged in a dogfight in which he shot down one of five German Fokkers attacking him, he was shot down, and crashed not far from Bar-le-Duc. He died on 19 May from his severe injuries, in Vadelaincourt military hospital in eastern France.

A sad, though courageous finalé, for a champion driver.

ABOVE LEFT:
Gordon Bennett Cup. Paris, Bordeaux
29th May 1901

ABOVE RIGHT:
Gordon Bennett Cup. Paris, Bordeaux
29th May 1901

RIGHT:
Leon Thery. Winner of The Gordon
Bennett Cup at the Circuit Auvergne
Michelin 5th July 1905

OPPOSITE PAGE:
Christian Lautenschlager in his
Mercedes at the 1908 French Grand
Prix at Dieppe

THE INTER-WAR YEARS

During the war, some drivers had continued racing in America at the Indianapolis 500, and this tradition continued once the war had ended. Europe was shell-shocked, weary and devastated, and it was only in 1921 that the Grand Prix returned to excite European enthusiasts once more. But how would European car manufacturers fare after years of being out of the loop? The answer was, surprisingly well. Unsurprisingly, perhaps, an American Duesenberg, driven by Jimmy Murphy, was the first car over the line after 30 laps, having covered the course in four hours and seven minutes, with the Italian-American Ralph DePalma coming in second in his French Ballot, fifteen minutes behind. (Édouard Ballot was a well-known engine designer, who helped Ettore Bugatti develop his first engines.)

The 1920s ushered in exhilarating developments in the world of Grand Prix racing. The first Grand Prix competition held outside France took place in Italy in 1921, and it was followed in later years by Spain, Belgium, and then Britain in 1926. And changes in the sport were not only happening in the field of car design and engine construction. New circuits were being constructed all over Europe that were much shorter in length; the 1921 Italian Grand Prix was held on one of these. In 1922, the Commission Sportive Internationale (CSI) was given the authority to regulate Grand Prix racing on behalf of the AIACR. That same year, a 2-litre engine capacity limit was introduced, so it was back to the drawing board for the designers.

One name, one engine design, began a short domination of Grand Prix racing for the second half of that decade, one of those names that sets motor enthusiasts' hearts beating a little faster; Ettore Bugatti. With drivers such as Louis Chiron and Tazio Nuvolari at the wheel, Bugatti swept the board every year for five consecutive years between 1925 and 1929 in the Targa Florio in the hills around Palermo in Sicily, Italy. The surge began in 1926; in 1927 they won twenty-three of thirty-one races, and the success continued throughout 1928 before slowing in 1929 and ebbing with the arrival of the thirties. When questioned about his dubious braking system, Bugatti is quoted as saying, *"I build my cars to go, not stop"*. That he certainly did. It was a phenomenal achievement attained with beautifully designed bodywork as well, and the Bugatti Type 35 went on to become one of the most successful cars in history. It was developed by Bugatti and Jean Chassagne, his master engineer and a racing driver, who also drove the Bugatti for the Type 35's first ever Grand Prix, in Lyon in 1924.

"The road holding was fantastic... the precision of the steering was something fantastic", said one of the men who got behind the wheel in 1930, René Dreyfus. It was envied by all.

Staggered starts became a thing of the past, too, abandoned in 1922 in favour of the mass start, which made its debut in the French Grand Prix in Strasbourg. In 1925 came another major change; and not for the first time it was brought about because of a death on the track. The English mechanic Tom Barrett was riding in a Sunbeam car — the first British car to win a Grand Prix race, incidentally — with driver Kenelm Lee Guinness, for the San Sebastian Grand Prix in 1924. On lap eleven, Guinness's car hit a rut, spun around and tipped over, throwing the two occupants into a railway cutting. Tom Barrett was killed instantly. In shock, Guinness never raced again. It was a moment of decision for the sport. No longer would mechanics be allowed to ride in a Grand Prix car. Tom Barrett's tragedy undoubtedly saved the lives of many future mechanics.

Mercedes-Benz were again responsible for innovation, this time off the track, when they introduced a system of flags and boards to relate tactical information to their drivers. It had been invented by their racing manager Alfred Neubauer. They tried out this system in the 1926 Solituderennen near Stuttgart in Germany.

By 1928, the strict 'formula' of restrictions on engine size and vehicle weight that had guided the Grand Prix races since their inception, were all but discarded, heralding an era that became known as Formula Libre; as the name indicated, there were practically no limitations for these competitions. One year later, the number of Grand Prix competitions had increased, so at the beginning of a new decade, motor racing was in a healthy situation. One proof of this was the introduction of the AIACR European Championship in 1931; for the record, it was won by Ferdinando Minoia driving for the Alfa Corse team.

When the drivers lined up at the start of the Monaco Grand Prix of 1933, they had taken part in qualifying laps for the first time, so that the fastest qualifying speed would be rewarded by a pole position on the grid. Racing was gradually taking a shape familiar to the modern world.

The early years of the thirties were in the grip of the Great Depression. Understandably, interest in motor racing declined somewhat. Nevertheless, the racetrack produced a legendary driver, the Italian Tazio Nuvolari, **"Il Mantovano Volante"**, **"The Flying Mantuan"**, whose victories in his Alfa Romeo were thrilling to watch. European Champion in 1932, then during a two-year hiatus in the European Championship, he won seven Grands Prix in 1933. In 1935, he was triumphant in a four-year-old Alfa Romeo against nine German cars. Without doubt, one of the greatest drivers of his day; no less a person than Auto Union designer Dr. Ferdinand Porsche said so and he should know. Nuvolari changed to Auto Union (later Audi) in 1938.

With Hitler ensconced in power in Germany, a new nationalism had been injected into the country, and Mercedes and Auto Union were being encouraged to build ever more sophisticated cars to prove the superiority of German craftsmanship. And the two teams didn't let the Führer down. Well, you wouldn't, would you? Initially producing sleek, aerodynamic machines that could exceed 175 mph (Mercedes would develop cars with 600bhp and top speeds reaching 200 mph before the decade was out), between 1935 and 1939 they dominated the European Grand Prix finish line, claiming a host of championships; there were eighteen Grands Prix by 1934. The Auto Union cars boasted V16 4.4-litre supercharged engines requiring special fuels concocted according to highly secret formulae. A four-wheel independent suspension used by both cars, was then swopped by Mercedes for a De Dion system, with rear leaf springs later being replaced by a torsion-bar suspension.

This was the golden age of the mighty 'Silberpfeile', the 'Silver Arrows', the nickname given to the German cars in 1934 because the aluminium body had been left unpainted to reduce the weight. Legend has it that they were 1.656 lb (1 kg) too heavy, and both Alfred Neubauer, the racing manager, and driver Manfred von Brauchitsch claimed the idea as their own. Fame is, indeed, a seductive lady. Manfred von Brauchitsch, Hermann Lang and Rudolf Carraciola were the drivers who could always be seen behind the wheel of a Silberpfeil in those heady years that produced some of the greatest cars ever made, with one of Britain's greatest pre-war drivers, Richard Seaman, getting a look in on three occasions, too. In fact, to the great delight of the German fans, he took the Silberpfeil to victory in the German Grand Prix in 1938. Tragedy awaited

Seaman, however, because in 1939 during the Belgian Grand Prix, he crashed his car into a tree. The engine burst into flames and the unconscious driver was so badly burned, that he died of his injuries just a few hours later. Reading of his death becomes unbearably poignant when we are told that his last words were; *"I was going too fast for the conditions — it was entirely my own fault. I am sorry"*. He was just 26 years old.

Grand Prix motor racing is, indeed, an unforgiving mistress.

With the war to end all wars still vivid in the memory, a few people now decided that sending people off to fight was even more exciting than motor racing, so everyone drained their beers and went off to slaughter each other again.

Motor racing in Europe came to standstill once more, in 1939.

As in WWI, many drivers didn't return to their cars after the conflict ended; amongst them were Jean Trenoulet, a French resistance fighter, who died on the 13th October 1944, Luis Fontés, who died on the 12th of October 1940 when his Wellington crashed, Ulli Bigalke, who died in his Luftwaffe plane, André Embiricos, who died on the 23rd of May 1941, killed during a naval battle off Crete and Ernst Günther Burggaller, killed in an accident in his Messerschmitt on the 2nd of February 1940.

Ettore Bugatti

ABOVE:
James Anthony Murphy at the 1921
French Grand Prix

RIGHT:
Henry Segrave and James Anthony
Murphy at the 1921 French Grand Prix.

FAR RIGHT TOP:
Jimmy Murphy in his Duesenberg at the
1921 French Grand Prix at Le Mans

FAR RIGHT MIDDLE:
Albert Guyot at the 1921 French Grand
Prix

FAR RIGHT BOTTOM:
Duesenberg at the 1921 French Grand
Prix at Le Mans.

A BRIEF PERIOD OF ADJUSTMENT

Miraculously, in 1945, having seen their factories first of all converted to military production and then heavily bombed during the war years, car manufacturers began motor racing on the Continent again in September 1945. And once again, it was car-crazy France that took the lead, so to speak, organising three races along a circuit in the Bois de Boulogne in Paris. Fittingly, the initial competition was a memorial race for a trophy named after Robert Benoist, a driver for Bugatti before the war, who had been shot by the Gestapo in 1944. (Benoist, and two other drivers, William Grover-Williams and Jean-Pierre Wimille, joined the Special Operations Executive (SOS) as secret agents. Grover — Williams was also executed.)

The races were won by a hybrid Simca/Fiat, a Maserati, and there was a highly emotional win, for the spectators and Jean-Pierre Wimille, who had had surged forwards, unstoppable, in a 4.7-litre Bugatti T59. Is it too sentimental to believe that he was determined to win, as a memorial to his SOE friends? Whatever the reason, Benoist and Grover-Williams would have been proud of him.

Those post-war years were glory years for the Italian cars, with Maserati and Alfa Romeo powering around the circuits and boasting some of the great names in racing at the wheels of their masterpieces of engineering; Alberto Ascari, Luigi Villoresi, and, of course, the inimitable Juan Manuel Fangio. These years also brought forth classic, wheel to wheel contests between the great cars of the day, Maserati, Ferrari, Talbot and Alfa Romeo, and they were the years in which spectators could delight in the feverish activity at the regular fuelling stops, which had by now been honed to a fine art and were all over in twenty seconds or less.

Leaving the war years behind them, the racing fraternity formed The Fédération Internationale d'Automobiles (FIA) to organise international motor racing events, and in 1947 the formula agreed upon permitted 1.5-litre supercharged or 4.5-litre non-supercharged cars. As the decade progressed, one by one the old Grand Prix tracks were put back into order; in Italy in 1947, the Italian Grand Prix was held at Milan until it could finally return to it's Monza home in 1949. The German Grand Prix returned to the Nürburgring in 1950 once the damage caused by the American 11th Armored Division tanks had been repaired.

1947 also brought with it a major change in the regulation of the Grand Prix competition. In that year, the formalisation of the World Drivers' Championship was agreed; several of the national Formula One Grands Prix would form the basis of a World Championship for drivers. Although three more years were to pass before the first official race took place, F1 regulations were followed from then on.

The 1940's bade farewell to a legendary car maker when Ettore Bugatti died in a Parisian military hospital from a lung infection on August 21 1947; but the decade said hello to what was to become an equally famous name in 1948, when Enzo Ferrari, who in 1929 had started his own firm, Scuderia Ferrari, entered the Grand Prix fray, winning the Circuito di Garda in October. The following year, 1949, the Ferrari crossed the line in first place on four occasions, stating firmly that here was a name to watch. It was in an open Ferrari 166C in 1948 that the legendary driver Tazio Nuvolari drove the race that endeared him to everyone and had Enzo Ferrari, with tears in his eyes, pleading with the seriously ill driver to quit as his car fell to pieces around him. Undaunted, only a broken spring prevented Nuvolari from gaining a spectacular victory. He had been part of, and now he witnessed the end of, an extraordinary epoch of motor racing.

As the 1950s dawned, so, too, did a thrilling new chapter in the story of Grand Prix racing.

RIGHT:
1927, Robert Benoist in his Delage after his victory at Monza

ABOVE:
Stirling Moss of Great Britain being wished good luck by his father former Brooklands driver Mr Alfred Moss before taking part in the 250 mile Grand Prix race at Silverstone aerodrome near Towcaster in Northamptonshire. It is the first recognised Grand Prix in Britain since before the Second World War and Stirling Moss is the youngest driver in the 500 cc race, 2nd October 1948

RIGHT:
A British ERA racing car, driven by G Ansell mid-air during a crash at Silverstone Grand Prix ciruit, Northamptonshire, 2nd October 1948

British GP at Silverstone, 1949

FORMULA ONE COMES OF AGE

The 1950 Grand Prix season, which included the inaugural FIAA World Championship of Drivers, began on 13 May and ended on 3 September. This would be a spectacular year for Alfa Romeo, as they won all six of the European Grands Prix. The points system initially gave eight points to the winner of each qualifying round, six to the second-placed car, four to the third, three for the fourth, two for the fifth and an extra point for the driver of the fastest lap. Ferrari had decided to use un-supercharged engines that year, and Aurelio Lampredi produced a 12-cylinder Ferrari that developed 300bhp at 7300rpm. Ferrari made their World Championship debut at the Monaco Grand Prix, but the decision to change engines had no impact on the championship table, because it was Alfa Romeo who homed in on championship victory with Guiseppe Farina at the wheel. Alfa took the championship again in 1951. The driver this time was to dominate the Grands Prix of the 1950s from then on; his name was Juan Manuel Fangio. An Argentinean nicknamed, 'El Maestro', Fangio is still revered and considered by many to be the greatest driver of all time. It was Fangio's last race behind the wheel of an Alfa, and it was the year that Ferrari's technical developments began to reap rewards; they won three victories that year — Alfa won four — and those wins signalled the end of track dominance by Ferrari's arch rival.

Fangio's last race of the season, to take the championship for the first time, took place at the Spanish Grand Prix, and it was Alfa Romeo's decision to use 18-inch tyres that won the day. Ferrari had chosen 16 inch... and spent a great deal of the race changing tyres because of tread problems. As a result, Fangio won with relative ease.

So few people had registered for the Formula 1 races that it was decided to run Formula 2 competitions in 1952 and 1953 instead; Formula 2 rules limited engines to 2-litre naturally aspirated, or 750cc supercharged cars. The steering of those racing cars in the early 1950s was still heavy and imprecise and therefore demanded great strength from a driver. A momentary miscalculation, or an irregular engine stroke in a bend, would instantly have the car in a spin. But developments were taking place continuously, and in 1951, one of the new technological advancements was introduced at Indianapolis; the revolutionary disc brake system. On the road, the style that drivers used to take corners as fast as they could involved no brakes at all, if possible, and was known as the **"four wheel drift"**. The driver would adopt a slightly longitudinal angle to the corner and as the wheels began to lose traction on the road surface they would be controlled by throttle and steering alone.

Ferrari took the limelight in spectacular fashion the following year, banishing Alfa from the podium completely and sweeping the Grand Prix board. They almost achieved the same feat in 1953, again with Alberto Ascari at the wheel, winning all but one of the European Grands Prix, yielding just the final race of the season at Monza in Italy to Fangio, now driving a Maserati.

And for the next four seasons, Fangio was the man you wanted behind the wheel of your car. If he was, you would be victorious and Ferrari, Maserati and Mercedes drove victorious Grands Prix with him ensconced in their shining automobiles. It was an extraordinary achievement by the Argentinean; five championships, a record only broken by Michael Schumacher forty-seven years later. Fangio was ten years older than the German driver would be when the record was broken.

That final race of 1953 in Monza announced the return of Fangio to the top of the class. It started off as a four-way struggle between Fangio, Ascari, Farina and Onofre Marimón. (Sadly, Marimón would become the first driver to be fatally injured at a Grand Prix World Championship, when he was killed on 31 July 1954 during a practice run for the German Grand Prix.) For 46 laps, these four were never more than twenty metres apart, and there were twenty-six changes of leader. The final lap was one of those breath-taking finishes that motor racing can deliver to the spectators, five drivers hurtling down the track together with Fangio behind Ascari and Farina as they approached the last corner. Overtaking and under pressure, Ascari suddenly spun out of control at the last corner, and Farina, in the effort to avoid him, ran onto the grass. Fangio, with lightening reactions, darted through unscathed and shot over the finish line. Ascari became the Grand Prix winner for the second consecutive year with 34.5 points. Fangio

in second place had 28; a new motor-racing hero was soaring upwards.

Incidentally, a young Englishman driving a Cooper Alta came in uncerenomiously at number thirteen that year. He would later be described as *"the greatest driver never to win the World Championship"*. His name? Stirling Moss.

The reign of un-supercharged 2500cc cars arrived in 1954. Fangio had been hired by the feared Silver Arrows team of Daimler-Benz, but their powerful giants didn't appear until July the 4th that year, so he began by driving the Maserati. He was immediately successful in the first two Grand Prix of the season in Argentina and Belgium. In July, the new W196, eight-cylinder Mercedes-Benz cars were available and three of them lined up for the start, with Fangio in one of them, accompanied by Karl Kling and Hans Herrmann in the other two. It must have been an imposing, if not fearful sight for the other drivers. And they had reason to be worried, because even though Herrmann managed to over rev his engine and blow it up on lap seventeen, (by which time Mike Hawthorn had also blown up his Ferrari engine) by then, he had broken the lap record. Fangio and Kling had smoothly gone to the front. And there they stayed, side by side, battling for the lead all the way to the finishing line where the team ordered Kling to take second place. Thus, Fangio won a punishing race in which only six cars finished. British driver Mike Hawthorn, in fact, came third in the table that year, but Fangio had streamed away to win the championship with 42 points. Fangio won all except the Spanish Grand Prix, in which he had been beaten by Mike Hawthorn putting in one of the best performances of his career in his Ferrari. It was a thrilling duel between the two of them, until loss of oil finally defeated Fangio. Maserati, Ferrari and Mercedes; these were the almost unbeatable teams of the 1950s; Mercedes won twice, Ferrari four times and Maserati also won twice between 1952 and 1959.

This fierce competition meant that there was much to look forward to in the 1955 season. Stirling Moss was now Fangio's teammate at Mercedes alongside Kling and Herrmann. Everyone anticipated a great contest with Grands Prix that would

Stirling Moss

have them on the tips of their toes.

It turned out to be a year of horrific tragedies, one of the worst seasons the sport has ever known.

American driver and double winner of the Indianapolis, Bill Vukovich was killed in May; another American, Manny Ayulo, had died just two weeks before. The celebrated Italian driver Alberto Ascari died testing sports cars at Monza, having ignored the warning when he had crashed into the harbour at Monaco four days earlier. His death was so upsetting it caused the Lancia team to close down their motor racing enterprise, and all their equipment was handed to Ferrari. On June 11 at the Le Mans 24-hour race, an even worse disaster struck. Mike Hawthorn had slowed down as he cut into the pits in his Jaguar D-Type, forcing Lance Maklin in his Austin Healey 100 to take evasive action and swerve, which kicked up a dust cloud and put him into the path of Pierre Levegh's Mercedes. Levegh had no time to react. He struck the Austin Healey at 150 mph (240 km/h) and the Mercedes scythed up into the air before hitting a retaining embankment and disintegrating. Chunks of metal and engine parts burst into the air and were hurled into the onlookers, and when Levegh was thrown from his car, his skull was crushed on impact with the ground and he was killed. As the magnesium-rich metal alloys ignited, white-hot flames swallowed the Mercedes, and the result of the conflagration and the shrapnel effect of the metal resulted in eighty-three spectators being killed and over one hundred injured.

The French, German, Swiss and Spanish Grands Prix were cancelled, before Fangio finally claimed his championship having won four of the six races. He never raced at Le Mans again. The sport was banned, and is still banned, in Switzerland, and the Pedralbes course in Spain was never used again.

The tragic veil thrown over the season rather overshadowed a thrilling success for one man. Stirling Moss beat Fangio, to the delight of the home crowd, in the British Grand Prix on 16 July. Moss had also driven the fastest round in 2.00.4. Fangio always maintained that Moss had simply been the better driver on the day.

A final consequence of this appalling season was that Mercedes followed Lancia's example and withdrew from motor sport but for an unspecified

Jack Brabham

time. The highly successful and advanced engineering of the Mercedes constructors, fifteen Grand Prix cars in the Formula One period with twelve first places in fifteen races in two Formula One seasons, would not be revived in circuit racing until the 1980's. Only in 2010 did Mercedes GP enter the F1 table again as an independent team with Nico Rosberg at the wheel, although in 1998 a McLaren-Mercedes car would send Mika Häkkinen across the finishing line, victorious again.

With considerable relief and hopes for a better year in 1956, the German team's achievements were overshadowed, with a strong showing by British cars such as the Connaught Alta GP 2.5 L4 and the Vanwall 254 2.5 L4, driven by Colin Chapman and Mike Hawthorn amongst others. Mike Hawthorn also drove a BRM Type 25; it was very fast, the four-cylinder engine developed 270bhp at 8000rpm and it sported disc brakes, but suffered from beginner's bad luck. Fangio was now with Ferrari, and Stirling Moss had moved on to Maserati, with whom he twice took victories from Fangio and ran the fastest lap three times over the season. With Fangio's teammate, the British driver Peter Collins, taking first place in two more races — one of which, the Belgian GP, riveted spectators with its wheel to wheel duel between Moss and Fangio — only Ferrari and Maserati got a look in this year. Fangio took a record third consecutive championship although with the least number of points he had ever attained, 30.

Those British Vanwalls provided some stirling opposition — yes, as you are asking, I did have to get that one in — in 1957, the season when Fangio won his fifth consecutive World Championship, this time in a Maserati. The British unleashed a formidable three-man team this year; Stirling Moss, Tony Brooks, and Stuart Lewis-Evans; what a team it was. Time and again it was Stirling Moss in his Vanwall who engaged the champion in the most nail-biting races of the season, robbing the Argentinean of three victories. But the excitement got to them on occasion: Moss was leading in the Monaco race but only got as far as the fourth lap before taking a chicane too fast and slamming into the barriers. His two British teammates seemed to think that Moss was enjoying some fun without them and promptly did exactly the same thing, removing all three cars from the race in one go. Taking the sense of British fair play a little too far, perhaps? That left the way open for Fangio to take another victory. That race was also notable for the interesting finish by an Australian driver, who would make his name in later years, to take sixth position; Jack Brabham had to push his Cooper Climax T43 over the finish line when his car

developed a blockage in the petrol tank. He wouldn't have to wait long for his moment in the sun, though.

All those who know anything about motor racing accept that that the Grand Prix in Germany turned out to be the greatest race in Fangio's extraordinary career. And as fate would have it, he battled for supremacy in the race that would make history, against the young British drivers Mike Hawthorn and Peter Collins in Ferrari 801s. For Fangio, it would prove to be the race of his life in his Maserati 250 F. He chose to start off with a half-full tank and soft tyres, and the pit stop almost proved to be his undoing when the wheel nut rolled beneath the car and couldn't be found for thirty agonising seconds. He finally emerged forty-eight seconds behind Collins, who was in second place. Not only did he catch up to Hawthorn, he overtook him on the twenty-first lap, and in the course of a fierce battle with him, in which Fangio was almost overtaken, he broke the lap record nine times. Nine times! And Collins had already set a new lap record of 9 minutes 28.9 seconds. By the end of the race, Fangio had reduced that to 9 minutes 17.4 seconds. It was an extraordinary feat of driving. The Argentinean knew that his had been an astounding victory. After the race he said, *"I have never driven that quickly before in my life and I don't think I will ever be able to do it again... I had never before had the courage to push things so far"*. A tribute, too, therefore, directed at the two British drivers who had inspired his magnificent win. Fittingly, Hawthorn and Collins came in second and third with Stirling Moss in fifth position. It had been a good day for the British cars and drivers. They had staked their claim and would not long remain without victory. And for the first time since the start of the series, Ferrari did not win a single World Championship race that year.

If 1957 had been a year of superlatives for Fangio, 1958 must go down in the annals of British racing history as one of the most extraordinary ever. Looking at the table of GP winners for that year, there were only two non-British drivers in the list, the American Jimmy Bryan and French driver Maurice Trintignant, and even he won the Monaco Grand Prix in a British Cooper Climax. Holland, Belgium, France, Morocco, they fell like dominos before the mighty British wave as Stirling Moss, Mike Hawthorn, Peter Collins, Roy Salvadori and Tony Brooks swept all aside that dared challenge them. They occupied the first five places in the championship table, with the American Harry Schell on joint fifth.

The incomparable Juan Manuel Fangio, the man that everyone praised as a driver and for his character, retired following the French Grand Prix in July,

probably understanding that his day was over and new lions were on the prowl.

One of those lions was, in fact, a lioness, Maria Teresa de Filippis. She was born in Italy on 11 November 1926 and on 18 May 1958 she made Grand Prix history by being the first woman to race in Formula One. She eventually participated in five World Championship Grands Prix.

The International Cup for F1 Manufacturers was awarded for the first time in 1958 — Vanwall won that inaugural Constructors' Championship — and although the formula for the engines was left unchanged, one major difference had been the reduction of maximum race lengths to 186 miles (300 km) or two hours, whichever came first. Specialised, alcohol-based racing fuels had been replaced because commercial petrol had become compulsory.

Even though Stirling Moss took four victories that year, he lost out by one point in the championship, to Mike Hawthorn, who brought home Britain's first World Championship title. The racing world was stunned by this British blockbusting performance. The Italians, in particular, must have wondered if they had woken up on another planet from the one they'd been on previously. Success had been achieved through one brilliant piece of design in construction; the British constructors had placed the engine in the centre of the car with the fuel tanks on either side, which rendered the car more responsive to the steering. Being able to dispense with the driveshaft meant not only a saving in weight, but it also enabled the driver to be positioned lower in the car and so improve the aerodynamics of the car body.

But it seemed as if the gods of fortune had decided that the glamorous young British lions were enjoying more than their fair share of glory. Tragedy had struck.

Blond and handsome, the epitome of a young athlete, Peter Collins, who, in the British Grand Prix less than two weeks before had taken victory in front of his jubilant home crowd, was killed in an accident at the German Nürburgring on August 3 when his Ferrari ran wide, left the track, hit a ditch and somersaulted on the eleventh lap. On 19 October during the Moroccan Grand Prix, Stuart Lewis-Evans lost control of the car when his Vanwall engine seized and he careered into a barrier where the car burst into flames. He died from his burns a week later.

Jim Clark

24

Luigi Mosso, Hawthorn's great rival, was also killed in 1958. He, too, had gone wide on a corner and hit a ditch, sending his Ferrari into a somersault.

Barely was the new year of 1959 underway before Mike Hawthorn was taken, killed in a road accident near London on 22 January. All the more poignant because only a few days before, the new World Champion had announced that at the age of 29, he was retiring from racing, still devastated by the death of his good friend Peter Collins the year before.

There was a new name in the game in 1959; the first United States Grand Prix took place at the Sebring International Raceway near Florida; it was won by New Zealander Bruce McLaren at the age of twenty-two; the youngest ever winner in Grand Prix history, a record that endured for almost five decades.

But the big news of the year was that Jack Brabham's hour had finally arrived, and with him, the car that would change motor racing, the rear-engined Cooper Climax T51. And he took the World Championship in 1959 even though he only won two races, with 31 points. He also made history when he ran out of fuel 500 yards from the line in the last race of the season at the American Sebring circuit and pushed his car over the finishing line.

Only Maurice Trintignant amongst the top drivers managed to complete every race. Aston Martin entered its DBR4/1 for the first time that year, but its designers seem to have been asleep because it was already out of date by the time it got to the track.

Jack Brabham took the championship again in 1960, this time not so much by default, but by superb driving in his Cooper-Climax T53, winning five of the Grands Prix, yielding just two victories to Stirling Moss in his Lotus-Climax, with another one going to American Phil Hill in his Ferrari, and one to Bruce McLaren. Two notable incidents that year were that John Surtees, a motorcycle champion, had tried his hand at motor racing in the British Grand Prix, coming in second, and Stirling Moss had been badly injured in a practice accident in which his half-shaft failed; the accident prevented him from competing in many more races that year. Just a quick mention that on the technical side, 1960 saw the end of the 2.5-litre Formula One, and the front-engined Formula One car was relegated to racing history.

With the winning driver now awarded ten points, Ferrari raced back to victory the following season, although it proved a rare exception to a trend that had already started and would continue; the predominance of British-manufactured winning cars. The Italians swept the board that year losing out on just three races, to win their first F1 constructor's title. Their driver, Phil Hill, won the Championship with 34 points, the first American to do so. His teammate, Wolfgang von Trips, had won two races, had 33 points, and needed just third place to win the championship before he was killed in the penultimate race in Italy; an accident that also took the lives of fifteen spectators. Von Trips had hit the car driven by an up and coming young British driver; .

Scotland's Jim Clark burst into the public's consciousness in 1962, when the Grand Prix season became a fierce duel between Clark and England's Graham Hill. Ferrari were once again wiped off the motor racing map; by Clark's Lotus-Climax 25 and Hill's BRM P56, and the two drivers shared seven victories between them with only Bruce McLaren and Dan Gurney managing to squeeze in one win apiece. But this was to be Graham Hill's World Championship, the man who had only passed his driving test at the age of 24. Hill's son Damon, would many years later also take a Grand Prix championship, making them the only father and son ever to do so, although his father was sadly no longer alive when Damon became World Champion. Amongst the celebrations in the British camp there was also a sense of sadness when it was announced that Stirling Moss would retire from racing. He had been badly injured in a serious crash at Goodwood and had required surgery. He recovered. Nonetheless, his eyesight had suffered, and he realised that he would never again achieve his former speed of reaction. A whole series of unfortunate incidents had denied Moss a World Championship that for a driver of his calibre should, by any criteria, have been his.

Jim Clark. The good-looking young Scot was now to see his bravery rewarded, and the measure of his World Championship win in 1963 can be taken by the fact that he had won the title by the end of his seventh race, out of a total of ten. It was another extraordinary season for the British, in fact; for the drivers, Clark and Hill it was almost a complete British whitewash. The only non-British team to cross the finishing line ahead of the other drivers was Ferrari, once, and even that car was driven by John Surtees.

The season was a more dramatic repeat of the previous one, with Clark and Hill battling each other for supremacy; but this time the roles were reversed. Graham Hill won the first race of the season. On his second outing, however, Clark showed what he was made of. In appallingly wet and rainy conditions and having started eighth on the grid, Clark had overtaken the entire field by lap seventeen, and he won the race 4.54 minutes ahead of Bruce McLaren in second place, as though he'd been driving through brilliant sunshine. Clark went on to take the championship with seven victories to Graham Hill's two, and John Surtees' single victory in his V6 Ferrari Type 156B in Germany. It was an astonishing season for the young Clark, who had become the first driver to win the Drivers' World Championship with three races still to go. Only in 1984 did Alain Prost equal Clark's record sequence of victories.

The Ferrari engineers must have breathed a sigh of relief the following year; finally, they were back in force with winning cars. Still, they didn't have it all their own way; the Brits were not going to give up without a fight, and Lotus, the new Brabhams as well as BRM, gave them a run for their money in a truly exciting four-way race. Jim Clark again won most races, three, with Graham Hill, John Surtees and the American Dan Gurney hot on his heels with two each.

When they arrived for the Mexican Grand Prix on October 25 1964, the drivers lined up for a finalé that thrilled spectators as one of the most riveting in Grand Prix history. Three drivers were in with a chance of victory; Graham Hill, Jim Clark and John Surtees. Surtees struggled for a long time on fifth place, but Hill's chances were severely curtailed when he was rear ended and spun around, although he managed to get back into the race. And then more bad luck, for Clark this time. With sixty of the sixty-five laps covered, Clark's engine lost oil and began to seize. On the penultimate lap he lost the lead, and when Surtees' teammate Bandini was ordered to allow Surtees over the line ahead of him into second place, Surtees had won his first, his only, World Championship. Clark was fifth in Mexico and Hill eleventh.

In the midst of all this drama, a young driver was sneaking up quietly on his peers; his name was Jochen Rindt. As it had for Clark, fame would soon come to the young German, too. But Clark, had to be beaten first, and he who had been robbed in 1964 flared back to glory in 1965. And he began the challenge for his second World Championship, by not competing in the second Formula One race, the Monaco Grand Prix, driving instead in the Indianapolis 500.

Lotus worked in tandem with the Ford Motor Company to produce a car in which Clark became the first European in nearly five decades to win this prestigious American race. The Lotus was a monocoque Type 38 with a Ford V8 motor that developed 495bhp at 8800rpm. The wider tyres now used on Grand Prix cars boasted just over 200mm surface contact, which was considered the optimum amount when paired with the smaller wheel radius. With the linings now made of nylon, the days of shredded rubber were far behind them. But the period of rapid advances in tyre technology, the battle for tyre supremacy, had not yet broken out.

Back in Europe, a strange sense of déjà vu had enveloped the Grand Prix season, because it was a breathtaking Clark and Hill wrestling match for all but two of the victories. Those rebellious two victories went to a newcomer driving a BRM; the newcomer was Jackie Stewart, who took his BRM to victory in Italy, whilst American Ritchie Ginther enabled Honda to get their noses into the Grand Prix in the last race of the season in Mexico.

Clark had the edge in this, the last 1.5-litre formula season, however, despite the Lotus team's problems with the newly developed Coventry Climax 32-valve motor, and he romped home with 54 points, Graham Hill taking second place with 40 and Jackie Stewart making his presence felt in his debut season, on 33.

So while all eyes were fixed on Jim Clark for the 1966 season, with perhaps a little side bet on Jackie Stewart or Jochen Rindt, no one saw the tenacious stalwart Jack Brabham revving up behind them. The 3-litre formula had now come into effect although only Ferrari, Cooper and Brabham were set up for it. The Brabham, designed by the driver himself, was now using a Repco V8 that produced 308 bhp at 8500 rpm, which made it the least effective of the cars that year. But it was Brabham who survived the deluge in Belgium that had cars spinning like tops, caused Jackie Stewart to crash and break his collarbone and Jim Clark to abandon the race because of mechanical failure. Jack Brabham won the race as he did in Germany in another downpour when he beat off the challenges by John Surtees, now in a Cooper-Maserati after friction with Ferrari, and Jochen Rindt, winning his first German Grand Prix in superb style. In total, Brabham won four races during a season in which no car completed every single Grand Prix race. Those four victories were enough to secure the championship for him for the third time at the age of 41.

Jacky Ickx made his debut in Germany this year. Ickx would go on to gain twenty-five Formula One podium finishes.

If anyone thought Jack Brabham was going to rest on his laurels they were seriously mistaken, because he was challenging hard for the championship again the next year and was, ironically, pipped at the post by one of his own cars driven by Denny Hulme from New Zealand. Hulme claimed that year's championship with 51 points to Brabham's 46.

And where was Jim Clark in all this? You can be sure he wasn't far away; he finished the season in third place, mainly because the new Lotus 49, although clearly a wonderful car, had teething problems.

Graham Hill, had decided that if Jack still had it in him then it was time

for a British **"vet"** to get another look in. It proved to be more than just a look in. Hill ended the 1968 season at the top of the table despite a run of bad luck, squeezing out the tenacious Jackie Stewart, who finished second. Stewart had missed several races due to injury. But as so often in motor sport, the joy of winning was dampened by tragedy. Those whom the gods love die young, and Jim Clark, who had looked set to storm through the season after winning the first F1 race of 1968, and thrill spectators for many years to come, was killed in a Formula 2 event at Hockenheim. He was thirty-two years old and had clocked up twenty-five Grand Prix victories thus beating the legendary Fangio's total.

Five drivers died that season, the last in which a track would be used without any safety modifications. As the last years of the decade approached, the times were, indeed, a changin'. Fire extinguishers became compulsory, and the cars had now begun to sprout wings to improve the aerodynamics (although the wings were briefly banned after they took to flying off by themselves!), and the old guard of drivers were rapidly losing ground to the hungry new upstarts, one of whom now staked his claim in spectacular fashion.

Jackie Stewart had been lying in Graham Hill's slipstream for long enough, and in 1969 he accelerated to the front of the pack in his new Matra MS80. Initially, his car's fins could increase or decrease their angle according to his speed, until legislation banned adjustable wings by the time of the third race in Monaco. Stewart won the first two races, was beaten one last time by Hill in the Monaco GP, then took the next three, the Dutch, French and British, before adding the Italian in September for good measure. Stewart's domination of the season was symbolised by the Barcelona competition, where he was two laps ahead of second-placed Bruce McLaren when he crossed the finishing line, an astonishing feat only equalled in 1995. Stewart took 63 points that season. Hill's efforts to maintain his mighty run at the top were dealt a severe blow when he was injured in an accident caused by one of his tyres blowing out. It was an omen; his illustrious career was almost over.

Graham Hill

ABOVE:
Argentine auto racer Juan Manuel
Fangio sitting at wheel of race car at Le
Mans

RIGHT:
Juan Manuel Fangio takes a corner in
his Ferrari-Lancia D50 on his way to
another victory at the The Syracuse
Grand Prix, Syracuse, 15th April 1956

ABOVE:
Phil Hill, Luigi Bazzi, Carlo Chiti and Dan
Gurney with the Ferraris in the pits during
the Portuguese Grand Prix at Monsanto,
23rd August 1959

LEFT:
British racing driver Stirling Moss (left)
adjusts the helmet of Ferrari driver Mike
Hawthorn (1929 - 1959) before a race,
1958

Jack Brabham in a Cooper Climax T55 at La Source hairpin, Belgian GP, Spa Francorchamps, Belgium 18th June 1961

Monaco GP in Monte Carlo, 1961

ABOVE:
Jim Clark, Zandvoort, Netherlands,
18th July 1965

RIGHT:
The Dutch Grand Prix; Zandvoort. Jim
Clark, Lotus 33, winning again,
18th July 1965

ABOVE:
Graham Hill and Jackie Stewart in BRM
P261s at the Monaco Grand Prix, May 1966

LEFT:
Jackie Stewart of Great Britain, (L) driver of
the Owen Racing Organisation BRM P83
BRM H16 talks with his team mate Graham
Hill before the start of the Italian Grand Prix at
the Autodromo Nazionale Monza near Monza,
Italy, 4th September 1966

Photographers stand close to the track as Jochen Rindt of Austria drives the Cooper Car Company Cooper T81 Maserati V12 during the XVIII BRDC International Trophy Race at the Silverstone Circuit in Towcester, Great Britain. 14th May 1966

Hockenheim, Germany. Spectators look at the wreckage of
the Lotus Ford Cosworth racing car in which former World
Champion Grand Prix driver Jim Clark was killed. Clark died
after hitting a tree during the German Grand Prix, April 1968

Italy's Lorenzo Bandini in a Ferrari crashes after losing control
at the chicane and the car ignites the straw bales causing a
fireball with Bandini trapped in the flaming wreck. Another car
approaching tries to pass the fireball, 9th May 1967

ABOVE:
Bruce McLaren getting new tyres while Chris Amon's Ferrari is about to leave the pits, France, Rouen, 7th July 1968

LEFT:
John Surtees in his BRM at the British Grand Prix, Silverstone, Northamptonshire, 1969. Mechanics work on the car while Surtees sits in the cockpit. John Surtees came to car racing in 1959 after a highly successful motorcycle racing career. He drove in Formula 1 from 1960 to 1972, winning 6 races and becoming World Champion in 1964 with Ferrari. Surtees drove for Honda in the 1967 and 1968 seasons. He formed his own team in 1970, which ceased competing in 1978. He spent only one season with BRM, the unreliable car failing to finish in half the races, including this one

TRAGEDY & TRIUMPH

What is there to say about the extraordinary season of racing that began a bright new decade? The new young hopefuls were out in force; the Scot Jackie Stewart, driving a March 701 owned by Ken Tyrell, Brazilian Emerson Fittipaldi in a Lotus-Ford, Austrian Jochen Rindt in the new Lotus-Ford 72,and Jackie Ickx in his Ferrari. It was going to be a cut-throat season. The new Brabham-Ford BT 33 was unveiled, with Jack now in his twenty-third year behind the wheel. The indefatigable Mr. Brabham even took victory in the season's initial Grand Prix in South Africa. It was the Australian's last race win.

There was a warning at the Spanish Grand Prix of what was to come, when Jackie Oliver and Jackie Ickx's cars both caught fire. The drivers escaped. And then Bruce McLaren was killed whilst testing a Can-Am car at the Goodwood circuit in southern England. But the show always had to go on, and Jochen Rindt suddenly burst into action showing why he was going to be the man to beat in the future, when he won five Grands Prix in six races. Rindt and Ickx had locked horns for the championship and carried the battle through onto the German course on August 2. A battle that Rindt won. The struggle for the championship was intense between the two rivals especially when Ickx took the next victory in Austria. Everything was shaping up for a classic showdown at Monza. And then this unforgiving sport ended another brilliant driver's life; Rindt suffered a brake system failure, causing his car to speed into and under a crash barrier during a practice run. He did not survive. At 28, the Grand Prix had claimed another of her heroes.

In deference to the young man's talent and sacrifice, Jochen Rindt was awarded the championship title posthumously. He was the only driver ever to be honoured in this way.

The scintillating four years that followed could best be described as the Stewart-Fittipaldi spectacular, although in 1971, Jackie Stewart took his second World Championship, his Tyrrell searing the race courses as he dominated the entire season, finishing on 62 points, far ahead of second-placed Ronnie Peterson on 33. Fittipaldi had to be content with sixth place. But he would have revenge in 1972. And how!

In the year in which the Brabham team was taken over by Bernie Ecclestone, a wealthy London businessman, Emerson Fittipaldi suddenly proved that he was a class act in his redeveloped Lotus-Ford 72D, winning five of the Grands Prix (Spain was only his second F1 victory, that is a measure of how his career had skyrocketed), although Jackie Stewart, who won four victories, fought him tooth and nail all the way. Stewart lost out to Fittipaldi at the British Grand Prix, coming in four seconds behind his rival after a high-octane jousting match at Brands Hatch. Fittipaldi took the crown in fine style with 61 points to Jackie Stewart's 45, becoming the youngest championship winner ever at the age of 25 years and 273 days.

The wet track at Monaco had shown that the super-wide tyres of the modern racing cars could not cope well with water, sending cars spinning almost on every lap. Some of the Surtees TS9 rims were eighteen inches wide, and the Lotus 72D had 14 inch tyres on the front and 9 inch tyres at the rear. Many of the cars that year had a great deal of the weight positioned over the rear axle, with wings mounted behind it. And this year saw the introduction of laterally drilled disc brakes, which were more effective at dissipating heat.

With Fittipaldi taking the first two victories of the New Year, Stewart had a fight on his hands; but the Tyrrell team needn't have worried, for in the season that saw the young James Hunt pick up 14 points, and the first appearance of a safety car, Jackie Stewart tucked five victories under his belt and 71 points, to win the championship for the third time. But his victory was shrouded in a familiar sadness, because Stewart's teammate Francois Cevert had been killed during practice for the US Grand Prix. Stewart was so distressed over his friend's death that after twenty-seven victories, he ended his career there and then, never racing again.

With Stewart no longer a rival, Fittipaldi might have been expected to have had everything his own way from then on. Not so, because not only was James Hunt chomping at the bit, Niki Lauda had arrived driving a Ferrari 312B3, in which he took pole position nine times in fifteen starts. This boy meant business.

Initially, his lack of experience showed, however, and the title eventually did go to Fittipaldi, who had changed to the McLaren team for the 1974 season.

Although Fittipaldi came second the following season, no one could have foreseen that he had won his last World Championship. In fact, no one could have foreseen the events of that season. It was the year Niki Lauda fulfilled his potential in brilliant style, his *"unbelievable year"* as he put it, in a Ferrari; the Ferrari 1312T, to be precise, a car that wiped the floor with its competitors, although it was not until the fifth Grand Prix in Monaco that car and driver gelled into a fearsome winning combination. As the season got under way, Fittipaldi continued where he had left off and won the first race. Lauda's Ferrari was nowhere, even though he had taken pole in Barcelona where the Italian Lella Lombardi gained the first women's point, coming in sixth.

And then, all of a sudden, the Ferrari was everywhere. Lauda took another eight pole positions and five victories. James Hunt managed to beat him to second position in Holland. Jochen Maas popped into the table on seventh place that year in his McLaren, as Lauda whipped his Ferrari around the course to take 64.5 points, seeing off Fittipaldi in second place on 45. It had been an astonishing year for the Austrian. The duel with Hunt proved prophetic, because these would be the two drivers to watch in the 1976 season.

The thrill of the 1975 season had only just ebbed away when driving legend Graham Hill crashed his Piper Aztec light plane. It was one crash too many, and one that he did not walk away from. One of Britain's legendary drivers was gone.

Lauda and Hunt delivered one of the most dramatic years of racing ever seen, in 1976. Lauda staked his claim early

Jackie Stewart

on with two emphatic wins and a second place in the US race. Hunt started his pursuit in Spain, where he was initially disqualified after he had overtaken Lauda halfway through and taken the victory. The offence? Apparently his car had been too wide; his points were only reinstated many months later. Hunt, who had eight pole positions that year, was disqualified on another occasion for driving illegally; i.e., swopping cars following a restart of the race during the British Grand Prix. Nothing could stop Lauda from gaining his second consecutive title, it seemed. Going into the German Grand Prix he had won five races to Hunt's two. That German Grand Prix will go down in history for the wrong reasons. On the second lap, Lauda's car started to spin. It hit the embankment and burst into flames and the Ferrari was then struck by two more cars. Trapped inside, Lauda inhaled toxic gases from which he went into a coma lasting for several days, and many feared he would not survive. His burns were appalling. With Lauda hospitalised, Hunt used the opportunity well and won four races. It was astounding that Lauda was back behind the wheel after just five weeks, determined to take the title; but he had really come back too soon, and he couldn't prevent Hunt from winning the championship with 69 points, just one ahead of Lauda.

One last note on the season; Jacky Ickx crashed in the US race and was fortunate to come out alive; after that he never seemed to recover his old form and enthusiasm, and left F1 for good in 1979.

Niki Lauda was still too good a driver to be denied for long, and with consistently strong performances in 1977, he took the World Championship for a second time, with 72 points. Hunt only managed fifth place, even though he had won three races compared to Lauda's two. But he had been forced to retire from eight races. The vagaries of the sport, however, meant that Lauda would not win the championship again until 1984.

Renault had now returned to the fold after an absence of seventy years, with a turbo-charged car. It may not have been too steady on its tyres, so to speak, but it was pointing

Niki Lauda & James Hunt

towards the future of car technology.

The number of Grands Prix in a season had now expanded considerably; there were sixteen races in 1978, and the stresses on car and driver were immense. Niki Lauda had changed to Brabham this year after friction at Ferrari, but this was to be the glory year for America.

Italian-American Mario Andretti had already made his presence felt for the previous two seasons in his Lotus, coming home sixth and third. Now he was to make that last leap to the top in his Lotus 79, which enhanced the so-called ground effect, whereby the underside of the car was shaped so as to generate as much downforce and as little drag as possible. Andretti took the first race in Argentina, and having been victorious in six races, won the championship with 64 points. The pinnacle achievement of a ten-year dream. No other American has won the championship since. His team, Lotus, took the constructor's title. Andretti was not completely spared the merciless sacrifices of the sport; his teammate, Ronnie Peterson, twice runner-up in the championship, the fastest man of his time, crashed his car at Monza. Hunt and two other drivers released him from the blaze, but the Swedish driver died later in hospital.

There were changes aplenty between 1979 and 1983; even the championship would change hands every year with a new name appearing at the top of the table each time.

Perhaps it was something to do with the impending ringing in of the new decade, but Lauda walked out on Brabham, and the glamorous, tousled James Hunt called it a day for his racing career. Australian Alan Jones raced himself back into the table for that last year of the 70's, and for Jody Scheckter, who been in the top ten ever since 1974, coming second in 1977, it was time to stand in the spotlight. Scheckter, despite an accident in Argentina, improved as the season progressed, driving with more focus and consistency. His teammate at Ferrari, Canadian Gilles Villeneuve, father of the future champion Jacques, who had entered the top ten the previous year, would come second this year, his highest ever placing. Villeneuve was just four points adrift, but had followed team instructions to allow Scheckter the title. It was just as well, for South African Scheckter abandoned F1 in 1980 and Ferrari plunged into the not-quite-good-enough abyss until the year 2000, when Michael Schumacher finally gave them another victory.

With the start of the 80s, came new faces to shuffle up the pack; and what skills and thrills the newcomers brought with them. The Brazilian Nelson Piquet climbed behind the Brabham wheel, and a talented young Alain Prost joined McLaren, although he would have to wait until the following season for his star to rise like Piquet's. But the star of the year 1980 was to be the Australian Alan Jones driving a Williams FW07 at first, and then the magnificent FW07B.

Skirted wings on cars were producing a downforce that enabled cornering speeds to rise alarmingly, and a driver could take three seconds from his lap speed of the previous year. The wheels now took corners as though they were on rails, which produced enormous tension in the outward-straining bodies of the drivers. The carbon fibre chassis, which reduced the possibility of chassis twist, had been introduced by Brabham the year before and would soon become standard on all cars; and the computer made its appearance when Tyrrell used one to monitor a new suspension system. It didn't help to produce any noticeable improvements in performance, however.

Alan Jones was given the fight of his life by Nelson Piquet, and with just two drives left before the end of the season, Nelson Piquet was one point ahead of the Williams driver; both men had three victories apiece. At Montréal, Jones forced his rival into the crash barriers and there was an enormous collision that led to the race being stopped. When it restarted, Piquet, in his spare car, had to withdraw when his engine failed, leaving Jones to take victory. There was bad luck for Piquet in the final Grand Prix in the United States, too, when he had to withdraw after 25 laps. Jones won the race and the championship.

Piquet's season came in 1981; he squeezed home by one point in front of the Argentinean Carlos Reutemann with whom he had fought a tyre to tyre race in a year that saw Alain Prost in his Renault rise threateningly to number five in the final table. After claiming his first victory in Dijon, Prost followed it with two more. The most exciting race of the season, however, involved Villeneuve, Jacques Lafitte, John Watson, Ello de Angelis and Reutemann in Spain. In this five-man tussle, Villeneuve proved that he still had the nerve of a Formula One champion and took the race.

With Ferrari, Ligier-Matra and Renault in the running this year and taking seven victories, the British manufacturers no longer had it all their own way. A new method had been found to counter the loss of downforce due to the removal of the skirts; hydraulic units were developed to lower the chassis as the car was in motion, so that standing still, the minimum required height of 60mm from the ground could be achieved. Gordon Murray, the Brabham designer, first introduced this innovation, which brought ground clearance to almost zero when the car was in motion. Unfortunately, the type of chassis required to cope with this was so rigid that driving a Formula One car had become a bone-shaking experience endangering the drivers' health.

Alain Prost began to climb the table inexorably, and it was just a matter of time before he tasted glory with a championship victory. But 1982 was to be a Williams' year again, this time with Keke Rosberg taking the winning chequered flag. This year was not without its difficulties, although it did see Niki Lauda re-enter the competition and the top ten table for the first time since 1978. Like a struck match, Rosberg flared once, before his career then died away. In a season when many drivers had claimed victories, he only won one race; the last time this had happened was in 1958 when Mike Hawthorn had pulled off the same trick to claim the title.

Difficulties had arisen off the circuit in rule disputes between two competing organizations, the Formula One Constructors Association (FOCA) and FISA, which had been stewing since 1979. There was a drivers' strike led by Niki Lauda against the so-called super licenses that Lauda felt would restrict a driver's freedom to change teams. There were disputes, too, over water-cooled brakes and when Ferrari used two rear wings, and there was a boycott of a FOCA team for the San Marino race. This all paled into insignificance when Gilles Villenueve was killed in the qualifying rounds of the Belgian Grand Prix after Jochen Maas had moved aside to let the Canadian pass only to find himself right in his path. The collision hurled Villeneuve out of his car and he died later that evening. Lotus boss Colin Chapman also died that year from a heart attack, and both Alan Jones and Carlos Reutemann decided to call it a day.

While Alain Prost went from strength to strength, there was a new kid on the grid in Formula Ford 2000. It would be a while before he made his presence felt, but Damon Hill would soon show the world that he had inherited his father's speed genes.

In 1983, Prost went head-to-head with Piquet for the championship in a contest that went right down to the wire in the last Grand Prix of the season in South Africa. At that point, Alain Prost was leading the championship with 57 points, and Nelson Piquet was just behind him with 55. Prost was fifth on the grid but fought his way up to third place before he was defeated by a turbo failure. Piquet took his second championship. He was the first driver to do so in a turbo-driven car, of which more had appeared that year; Alfa Romeo's V8 1497cc unit, and Honda's V6 engine could be seen at the Geneva Motor Show. These turbo engines were now developing between 700 and 800bhp in cars that the Formula One rules now dictated had to weigh at least 540 kg. But the turbo would not kick in for between half a second and one second after pressure

was applied to the pedal, a delay that could cause a car to slide when exiting a corner. Other new rules stated that the rear wings must be set at the maximum height of 100cm, although the width was restricted to 100cm, which reduced the downforce somewhat. But more rear wings with vertical side plates appeared this year, too, and these new wing designs helped to increase the downforce again. And the lightning fuel and tyre stops that Brabham had tried out the previous year had been so successful that all the other teams now did the same thing.

British driver Nigel Mansell had driven his Formula One debut in 1980 but had failed to make the top ten table; now, in 1984, he finally made it, and would not leave it until he retired in 1992, driving his Lotus 95T to a number nine place. On equal points, 13, was another new face in the table destined to become a legend, Ayrton Senna.

But the action at the top in 1984 was between Niki Lauda and Alain Prost and only a hair's breadth separated the two drivers — who were now teammates, both driving McLarens. With refuelling now banned (it would be made legal again in 1994), and turbocharged engines allowed to use just 220 litres of fuel per race instead of 250 (this 'handicap' was countered by chilling the fuel, which 'shrank' it, sometimes to below -50 degrees, and that meant that some 15 litres of additional fuel could be squeezed into the tank), all was set for a classic contest.

And it truly was a battle of the Olympians. Lauda and Prost; the two unyielding rivals jousted for victory over the last seven races giving no one else a chance. Prost won seven victories to Lauda's five. The championship came down to the competition in Portugal with Lauda ahead on points. The deciding race was as dramatic as anyone could have wished for; it all hung on just one half point. Lauda only needed a second place to secure the championship, but he was having trouble passing Nigel Mansell, until eighteen laps before the end. For Lauda, this could possibly have been the last bite of the cherry, which, indeed, it proved to be, as he came in tenth the following year before taking off his Grand Prix helmet for the last time. Prost grabbed the lead from Keke Rosberg in the Honda-Williams and held it through to the finish. But the final decision had lain with Nigel Mansell, because when he had spun out of control on the eighteenth lap, he had handed Lauda second place and, therefore, the championship.

Even though Ayrton Senna came home in joint ninth place with Nigel Mansell at the end of the season, both with just 13 points, he had gained his first honours amongst the big boys, and it was clear that here was a major new talent. Mansell had just squeaked onto the table by pushing his car over the line during the Monaco Grand Prix, and fainting as a result.

Over the course of the next three seasons, Senna began to put the notches in his exhaust pipe. The McLaren, too, driven by both Prost and Lauda in its TAG-Porsche engine version with twelve victories in sixteen championship races and later to become Senna's car of choice, was also going to prove hard to beat. It dominated the tables until Michael Schumacher came along in the early 1990s. The McLarens had been using Michelin tyres and they, together with all the other teams that had been using Michelin rubber, received a shock when the French firm said that it would no longer take part in Grand Prix racing.

On the track, following two years as runner up, the brief but exciting Alain Prost era had begun. The 1985 season, in fact, turned out to be one of the most nerve-wrenching there has ever been, according to ardent aficionados of the sport. Prost was made to fight for the title by the Italian Michele Alboreto in his Ferrari, who had soon racked up forty-six points from seven podium appearances. So Ferrari were looking like champions; at least until the Austrian Grand Prix. It was here, that Niki Lauda announced his retirement, and here that Alain Prost began his inspiring fight back.

Prost was on pole position, his average speed 155 mph. McLaren was king on the Österreichring — pardon the poetic lapse, but this was a year for poetry — in Austria, an extremely fast and scenic track. Lauda was unlucky when turbo failure forced his exit and Prost took the chequered flag first.

Stefan Bellof, a rising star of Formula One, was another of the many drivers who did not live long enough to fulfill their potential and died when they were off the Grand Prix track; Bellof was killed during the World Endurance Championships. The Dutch Grand Prix was the last one Bellof drove, and it was also the thirty-fourth and last to be held in the Netherlands; here, too, Niki Lauda drove his last winning race before he retired.

Despite Nigel Mansell putting in a great showing and winning at Brands Hatch, his first home victory, and in South Africa, it was Prost who put in the most victories, taking five by the end of the season in his McLaren MP 4/2B. And Prost took the coveted World Championship with 73 points, ahead of

Alain Prost

Alboreto on 53.

He repeated the trick the following year, chased all the way, this time by Nigel Mansell in his Williams, who was just two points behind him at the end of the season with 70. The talented Nigel Mansell would come runner-up three times before he was allowed to taste the sweetness of a championship winner's podium appearance. In 1986, everything had come down to the final race in Australia with Mansell favourite to win. But it was destined not to be; heartbreakingly for the British driver and his fans, Mansell's tyre blew out on the sixty-third lap.

Mansell's rival the following year would be his own teammate. Nelson Piquet had never quite gone away since his last victory in 1983. Having changed over to the Williams team in 1986, he was suddenly given a new lease of life and throttled his way back to the top in 1987. That year saw four drivers battle it out for top place; Prost, Senna, Piquet and Mansell. Mansell once again encountered bad luck; two retirements at Monaco and Detroit left him trailing, and when he crashed during qualifying and hurt his back, which put him out of the race at Suzuka in Japan, it ultimately cost him the championship, despite six victory podiums. Prost and the McLaren eventually wilted and finished the season fourth behind Senna with 57 points on third.

Senna was seemingly fearless and consequently took risks with his driving, which was absolutely breathtaking to watch but left many people wondering if the young Brazilian would always be able to escape an accident by a hair's breadth. This championship, however, was firmly in the hands of Nelson Piquet, whose consistency had brought rich rewards, and he won the title with two races still to go. And the rich rewards that motor racing could now bring, with television interest so high, meant that the top ten teams in each season would now be able to travel to the Grand Prix the following year free of charge.

Another Austrian, Gerhard Berger, had entered the top ten for the first time in 1986 and would stay around for many years challenging all those around him on the track, though he would never equal his countryman Lauda's record. In 1988, he was to rise to number three in a Ferrari, a position he would gain for a second time in 1990, although in a McLaren at that point, sharing the position with Nelson Piquet, another irrepressible driver. Berger chose the wrong year to peak, however, because Ayrton Senna was also on top form.

Turbocharged engines were making their final appearances this year of 1988, and would give way to the naturally aspirated engines in 1989. And Benetton began to taste success when their car, with a Ford DFR 3.5 V8 engine and driven by Belgian Thierry Boutsen, came in fourth.

It was an extraordinary season; the table shows that two men won every race except one, with Gerhard Berger snatching a victory at Monza in Italy. It is, perhaps, not surprising to learn that the two men were those titans of the track, Ayrton Senna and Alain Prost. These two extraordinary drivers would lock horns for the next four heart-pounding seasons. In 1988, that meant, that the year was practically a whitewash for McLaren-Honda, because Senna and Prost were now teammates. And when the season was over there were just three points separating them.

It was unfortunate for Prost that Senna was on unbeatable form and took home the greatest number of points ever in a Grand Prix season; 90. And the race that perhaps symbolised the Brazilian's extraordinary fierce determination was the deciding contest at Suzuka in Japan. A win here would guarantee Senna the title, but he began the race in fourteenth position because his car stalled, and it was only because of the sloping track at the start that he was able to stay in the race at all. It was an inspired piece of driving by the Brazilian, because by lap 27, he was in the lead. Not only did he stay there and take the race and the championship, he also drove three consecutive fastest laps and set a new lap record. He won eight of that season's races; Prost won seven. Had it not been for the rule that dictated that only the eleven highest scores counted, (no, best not to even think about it!) Prost would have won, having scored eleven points more. In 1964, Graham Hill lost the championship for the same reason, and the system was only changed in 1991.

All in all, then, a season to savour.

So what would happen the following year? Would the rivalry that had been sharpened by Prost's open criticism of Senna's driving now cause problems? Was Senna unreachable?

1989. The 3.5-litre atmospheric engines proved as fast as the 1.5-litre turbo engines, a fact which bemused everyone slightly. Gone was the turbo-lag effect, acceleration was admirable, 124.2 mph (200km/h) from a standing start in 5.2 or 5.3 seconds, and corners could be assailed more easily. Using the so-called **"Concorde beak"**, which was narrow and allowed for wider front wings, also became the norm for many designers. What was not to like? Nigel Mansell had driven some superb races the previous year and had now changed to Ferrari, where his skill was proving to be a threatening red devil to McLaren, although Italian Ricardo Patrese in a Williams beat him down to fourth spot that year.

Ayrton Senna

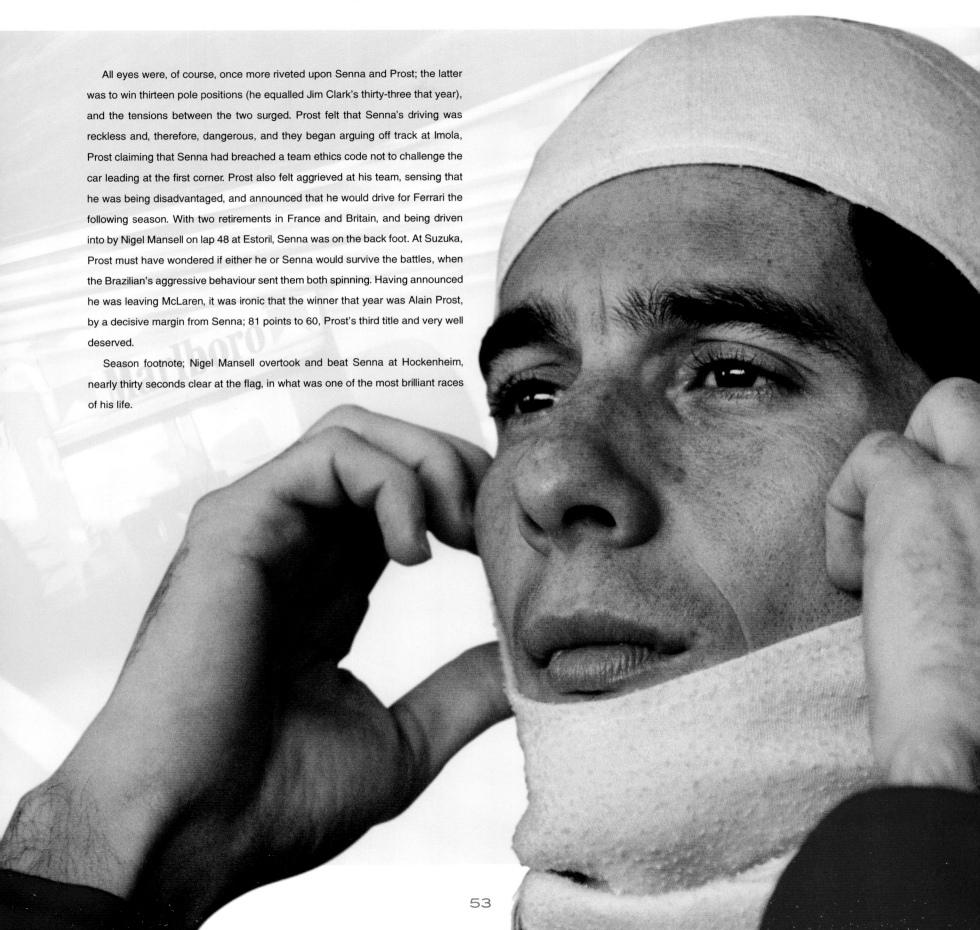

All eyes were, of course, once more riveted upon Senna and Prost; the latter was to win thirteen pole positions (he equalled Jim Clark's thirty-three that year), and the tensions between the two surged. Prost felt that Senna's driving was reckless and, therefore, dangerous, and they began arguing off track at Imola, Prost claiming that Senna had breached a team ethics code not to challenge the car leading at the first corner. Prost also felt aggrieved at his team, sensing that he was being disadvantaged, and announced that he would drive for Ferrari the following season. With two retirements in France and Britain, and being driven into by Nigel Mansell on lap 48 at Estoril, Senna was on the back foot. At Suzuka, Prost must have wondered if either he or Senna would survive the battles, when the Brazilian's aggressive behaviour sent them both spinning. Having announced he was leaving McLaren, it was ironic that the winner that year was Alain Prost, by a decisive margin from Senna; 81 points to 60, Prost's third title and very well deserved.

Season footnote; Nigel Mansell overtook and beat Senna at Hockenheim, nearly thirty seconds clear at the flag, in what was one of the most brilliant races of his life.

Jochen Rindt into Mirabeau corner. At the back the Hotel Metropol, Monaco, Monte Carlo, 10th May 1970

ABOVE:
Jochen Rindt in the pits with his wife Nina during his last practice session on Saturday, Monza, 6th September 1970

RIGHT:
Nina Rindt waiting for her husband Jochen to pass by. He died in an accident at Parabolica just moments after this picture was taken, Italian Grand Prix ,Monza, 6th September 1970

ABOVE:
Jackie Stewart in his cockpit, Dutch
Grand Prix, Zandvoort, Netherlands,
21st June 1970

RIGHT:
Jackie Stewart of Great Britain sits on
the wheel of his Elf Team Tyrrell 003
Ford Cosworth DFV before the start of
the Grand Prix of Monaco on 23rd May
1971

ABOVE:
The Belgian racing car driver Jacky Ickx
(Jacques Bernard Ickx) beside a Ferrari
312 B2 waiting the beginning of the
race during a break in the French Grand
Prix. Le Castellet, July 1971

LEFT:
Jacky Ickx in a Ferrari 312B in Monaco,
10th May 1970

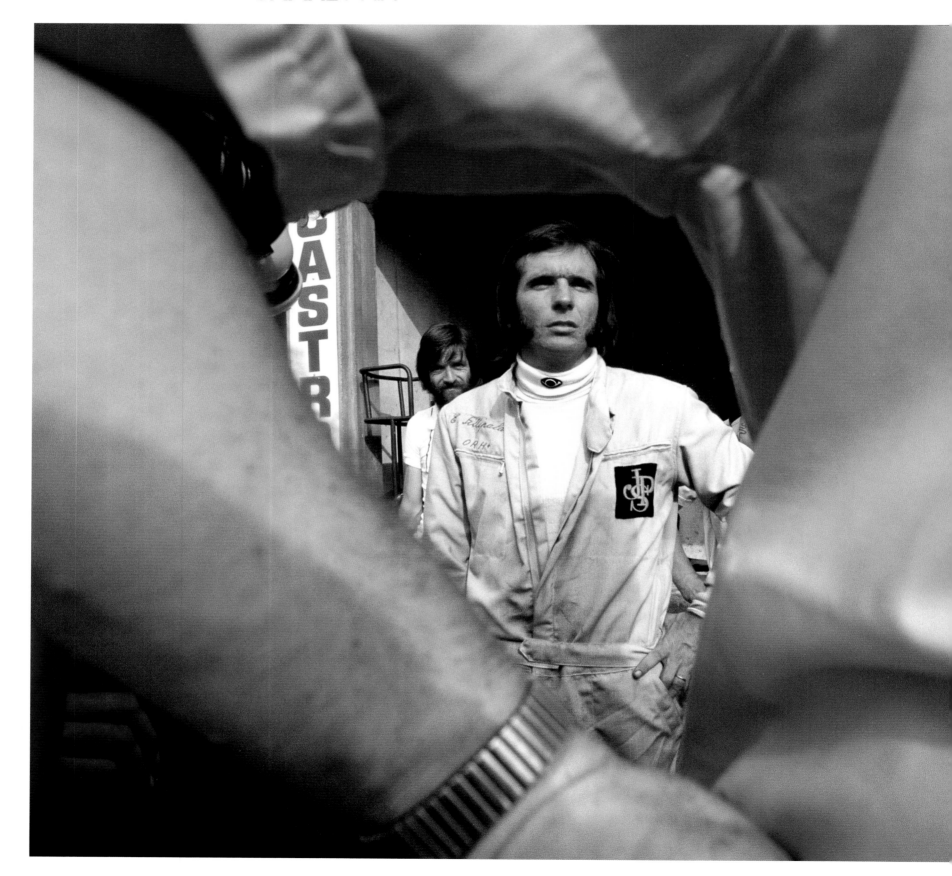

ABOVE:
Colin Chapman, team principal and owner of John Player Team Lotus (with clipboard) and Ronnie Peterson, driver of the John Player Team Lotus Lotus 72E Cosworth V8 during practice for the German Grand Prix at the Nurburgring, Nurburg, Germany. 2nd August 1975

LEFT:
Emerson Fittipaldi, Lotus-Cosworth 72D, Italian Grand Prix, Monza, 10th September 1972

ABOVE:
Sunday morning: Ferrari's polesetter
Niki Lauda at his car in the pitlane,
Spanish Grand Prix, Montjuich Park,
27th April 1975

LEFT:
Ferrari driver and championship leader
Niki Lauda, German Grand Prix,
Nurburgring, 3th August 1975

ABOVE:
James Hunt, winner of the British Grand
Prix, Brands Hatch, 18th July 1976

LEFT:
Niki Lauda of Austria, driver of the
Scuderia Ferrari SpA Ferrari 312T2
talks to rival James Hunt, driver of the
MarlboroTeam McLaren M26 Ford V8
before the start of the Belgian Grand
Prix at the Circuit Zolder in Limburg,
5th June 1977

ABOVE:
Bernie Ecclestone (middle) and Gordon Murray at Nelson Piquet's car in the pits, Austria, Zeltweg, 16th August 1981

LEFT:
Gilles Villeneuve gestures for adjustments to be made on the Scuderia Ferrari 312T4 as spectators look on during practice for the Grand Prix of Austria at the Osterreichring in Spielberg, 11th August 1979

Ayrton Senna of Brazil drives the Honda Marlboro McLaren MP4/4 Honda RA168E turbo during the Grand Prix of Monaco on 15th May 1988

IT'S TOUGH OUT THERE

For the next two years, Senna showed what a magnificent driver he was, taking the title in 1990 and 1991. Prost, now teammate to Mansell at Ferrari, was again hot on Senna's heels in 1990, the year that Adelaide was host for the 500th Grand Prix; the race was won by Nelson Piquet. Prost and Senna became untouchable and opened up a huge lead once more. Senna was a dangerous man to have on your tail, though, as Italian Alessandro Nannini found out when he and Senna touched as the Brazilian was trying to overtake and sent the Frenchman's Benetton into the air. Senna went on unscathed to win the race. Prost's turn to be on the receiving end came in Suzuka, when Prost got in front, and Senna, desperate to overtake, send the two of them off the track and in doing so, claimed his second title by default. We don't know what Prost thought, but it is certain that Senna's actions didn't endear him to anyone. It would not be the last time this dangerous scenario would occur in a Grand Prix.

Nonetheless, Senna was champion again the following year, again with a large number of points, 96, ahead of his new challenger, Nigel Mansell, on 72. Prost failed to win a Grand Prix for the first time since 1980. But Mansell, in a Williams by now, had given warning.

Frank Williams had only just managed to prevent the British driver from retiring, and how wonderful that he did so. Mansell gave the Brazilian a thrilling run for his money in 1991. In 1991, too, a young Michael Schumacher made such a great impression on the Benetton team that he was quickly put into one of their cars. For McLaren, it was a bittersweet triumph, because it would be another seven years before one of their cars again topped the championship table; Williams was the name to watch from now on.

And it was the Williams car that finally took Nigel Mansell through to glory. And what an astonishing season 1992 was for the British driver. It could not have been better if he had written the script himself. The list is remarkable; he became unbeatable in the first five Grands Prix of the season and clocked up 108 points and twelve podiums, a new record. He eventually took nine victories having been in pole position for every race except two, was in pole position and drove the fastest lap in four races, and came second in three races, retiring from the others. He was already champion after the twelfth Grand Prix in Belgium, won, incidentally, by Michael Schumacher, who finished the season third on 53 points; a long way behind Nigel Mansell, but it was already clear that here was a driver of exceptional talent. The British Williams-Renault, McLaren-Honda and Benetton-Ford cars wiped the floor with the competition; no other car took a Grand Prix title that year and they filled the first six championship places.

Silverstone was a special race for Nigel Mansell and he ran it in fine style. Although Patrese, now Mansell's teammate at Williams, squeezed past him, the Italian sportingly waved Mansell through on the straight, and once in the lead, Mansell was not likely to give it up. Behind him, Michael Schumacher was proving that he, like Senna, would take risks to get to the finish line when he tried to force his way into a non-existent gap and collided with Stefano Modena's Jordan. Schumacher came fourth, whilst his teammate at Benetton, Martin Brundle, after a terrific start eventually came in sixth.

But Silverstone was Nigel Mansell's dream come true, a victory on home turf in his championship-winning year, which also saw him beat Jackie Stewart's record as the most successful British driver; he now had twenty-eight wins to Stewart's twenty-seven. On top of that, Mansell had led every lap from pole position and set the fastest lap before winning; it was a Grand Slam for the British driver.

It was at this point that the sport showed that ecstasy and agony are never very far away from one another in motor racing; relations between Williams and Mansell froze when Williams signed Alain Prost, and the British driver learned that Senna also wanted to race with Williams. Williams, to their eternal disgrace, offered a deal to the champion driver that he was not prepared to accept. Rightly insulted, Mansell refused and decided that for him, Grand Prix racing was a thing of the past. It was a sad end to an exceptional year and an exceptional driver.

The first of this year's youngsters to watch was Damon Hill, making his debut in the Brabham car. Hill replaced the Italian driver Giovanna Amati, the fifth and last female driver to enter Formula One. Brabham was a victim of its financial difficulties and folded after the Hungarian Grand Prix. Then there was Mika

Häkkinen, who made it into the table in his second year in Formula One driving his Lotus, taking eleven points and coming in eighth. With Michael Schumacher already firmly established, the new champions were rising up through the ranks.

Alain Prost had taken a sabbatical year and was now back, driving for Williams. The rest must have done him a power of good because he now surged back to the top of the table for the fourth and last time in his illustrious career. His teammate was Great Britain's Damon Hill, and what a year he would have. A young Rubens Barrichello entered the Formula One circus for the first time and would continue to race until 2011. In 1993, his first races would be in the Jordan seat. A new team on the grid was the Swiss Mercedes-backed Sauber team. Another young driver in a Jordan seat in 1993, Edmund **"Eddie"** Irvine Jr. from Northern Ireland, debuted at the Japanese Grand Prix.

The scene was set for what became the final Prost-Senna duel. And the opening race in South Africa, the last of its kind there, set the pattern. It was a dramatic race. Prost was in pole position with Senna behind him, but after a poor start, he ended up behind Senna and Hill. The still inexperienced Hill spun his car, whilst Schumacher slipped through into second position. On lap thirteen, Prost was back in second place, attempting to overtake Senna, which he managed to do on lap twenty-five. Not to be outdone, Schumacher also passed Senna. After pit stops, Senna was back in the lead, and it was when Schumacher again attempted to pass him that he touched the Brazilian and put himself into a spin that took him out of the race. Senna eventually saw Prost take his first Grand Prix of the season.

Until the Hungarian Grand Prix, the races were a tug of war

Nigel Mansell

between Prost and Senna; Damon Hill broke the pattern. Hill had suffered a great deal of bad luck until then, including punctures and an exploding engine, but shone as he won three races back to back. Michael Schumacher won at Estoril in Portugal. It was Alain Prost's year, however, and he drove the Williams to a cracking total of 99 points, ahead of Ayrton Senna on 73, having taken seven victories. In 199 Grand Prix, Alain Prost had won a record 51 times. With his consistency of style, he was regarded as the best all-rounder of his generation.

The sport of motor racing has seen many heroes come and go, and many of those heroes offered their lives up to the thrill of the mighty Formula One engines, those demanding and uncompromising goddesses. They may not have gone willingly, but they weighed up the very considerable risks, and they decided to take them. Yet, when the tragedies that haunt the sport are spoken of, there is one year that holds particular poignancy in the hearts of all who love Formula One.

That year was 1994.

It had all the ingredients to become a classic battle of wills between the upstarts Damon Hill, Mika Häkkinen and Michael Schumacher and the exotic, unpredictable, glamour boy of the sport, Ayrton Senna. It evolved to become mired in controversy and tragedy.

Senna was now at Williams, partnered with rising star Damon Hill, and another young man who rose into the top ten that year, David Coulthard.

Many changes were introduced in an attempt to curb the excessive use of technology that many thought were making drivers nothing more than puppets. In particular there was a ban on electronic

Damon Hill

'driver aids'; active suspension, traction control, anti-lock brakes and launch control. Ironically, Ayrton Senna had commented that the season would be one with a lot of accidents because there had been no corresponding attempt to slow the speed of the cars. Refuelling was back, too, having last been used in 1983.

Michael Schumacher set down the markers from the start, winning the first two races and setting the fastest lap time on both occasions. Both Senna and Hill failed to complete the second contest.

San Marino, therefore, was an important race. It began under the most threatening of portents. Rubens Barrichello almost died in practice when he crashed at high speed. And during qualifying, the front wing came off the Simtek driven by the young Austrian Roland Ratzenberger, who was racing in his first F1 season. The car struck a wall at 195.7 mph (314.9 km/h), and Ratzenberger was dead before he reached hospital. It was Saturday 30 April 1994.

On 1 May, Senna took pole for the third time. After a shunt, the safety car came out for only the third time since its introduction in 1993, and with a rolling start, the race was under way.

Senna took the lead. After two laps, he came to the Tamburello corner at 190 mph (306 km/h) slowing to 131 mph (211 km/h).

And hit the concrete wall.

Part of the suspension struck him, and debris flew across the track. Ayrton Senna died in hospital. The shock waves were felt far beyond the world of Formula One. The sport had lost one of the most brilliant and successful drivers it has ever known.

Heinz-Harald Frentzen was given a Formula One drive for the first time that season, in Brazil. He had impressed Frank Williams so much that he was offered the seat that Senna had left. Frentzen decided to stay where he was for the time being.

The season then fell into a pattern of Schumacher first and Hill second, but Hill eventually took six victories, so the championship would be decided in Australia. It became infamous and itself set a pattern.

Schumacher went wide at the East Terrace corner on lap 35, and brushed the wall. Hill was right behind him and able to pass, so he took the inside line into the corner. Hill drew alongside Schumacher, who suddenly turned the Benetton

and aggressively struck Hill. Schumacher's Benetton became momentarily airborne and was out of the race. Hill's car, too, suffered damage and soon had to be retired. The incident looked deliberate, but it won Schumacher the race, giving aficionados a strange déjà vu sensation as it harked back to a previous year when a similar incident had given Ayrton Senna the championship victory over Alain Prost in 1990.

After the emotional roller coaster of the previous year, the 1995 season, though full of drama, fortunately produced none of the tragedies. Williams and Benetton carved up the first four places this season, and the two toughest sparring partners were again Michael Schumacher and Damon Hill. Despite Damon Hill's best efforts, however, this turned out to be Schumacher's most impressive outing to date, even though Hill won two of the first three races. Jean Alesi in a Ferrari, Johnny Herbert with Benetton, and David Coulthard also in a Williams, managed victories this season, but Michael Schumacher dominated with nine wins. Damon Hill took the chequered flag first on four occasions, but with 69 points at the end of the season, he was way behind Schumacher's 102.

The extent of Schumacher's dominance could be seen from his performance at Spa in Belgium, where he took the winner's podium from Hill by clawing his way back to the lead from sixteenth position. It was a masterclass in fearless, skilled driving. That rivalry between Hill and Schumacher was far from friendly; in fact, it was dangerous, as was proven at Monza when the two collided, yet again, on lap 23.

New technical regulations had been introduced this season following Senna's and Ratzenberger's fatal accidents; driver and car combined could now no longer weigh more than 1,312 lb (595 kilograms); the cars' ride height had been raised, the cockpit opening enlarged and the sides had been raised to provide better head protection for the driver; engine capacity had been reduced, fuel specifications were tested more rigorously and the size of the aerodynamic wings had also been reduced. And, inevitably, crash testing had become more stringent.

It might have seemed that the apparently aloof German driver was going to dominate the table from now on, but not so; Jacques Villeneuve, David Coulthard, Mika Häkkinen and Damon Hill had other ideas. At the end of the season, Schumacher changed teams and went to Ferrari, which, in the short term, improved the team's prospects greatly, but diminished the driver's.

Damon Hill found himself competing that year, not so much against Michael

Schumacher as against the son of another famous racing father, as he was himself. The Canadian Jacques Villeneuve was driving his debut season as Hill's teammate in the Williams, and he immediately staked out his claim to motor sport fame and glory. Fortunately, Hill was more than equal to the challenge, for he would not get a second shot at the target.

Hill set down the markers from the word go; he won the Australian Grand Prix — a milestone, as he had now equalled his father's fourteen wins — the Brazilian and the Argentinean Grands Prix back-to-back, setting a tough hill, (apologies!) for the Canadian to climb.

Villeneuve was not cowed, however, by the calibre of competition, and at the European Grand Prix, he took the lead and kept it all the way, taking the chequered flag less than one second ahead of Hill. It was nail-biting stuff. Hill had the, undoubtedly pleasurable, experience of taking on Michael Schumacher in pole position on two occasions and beating him both times. Ferrari, however, with Schumacher at the wheel, were flagging that they were back in business.

Villeneuve was proving hard to shake off, and with two races left to go, Damon Hill was only 13 points in the lead; and to make the final race even more of a death or glory show down, Villeneuve won the penultimate contest in Portugal; everything was down to the last race.

As it turned out, fate gave Hill a relatively easy ride, because Villeneuve crashed on lap 37. Damon Hill won the title and became the first son of a Formula One champion to take the trophy himself. With 97 points, followed by Villeneuve on 78 and Michael Schumacher on 59, Hill had decisively driven himself into the history books.

For 1996, sharp nosecone designs had ended their careers; blunter noses were the flavour of the season. Also, the cockpit sides had been raised again, to mid-helmet height, and there was a wraparound foam head restraint to prevent head injuries, such as those Mika Häkkinen had suffered in 1995.

Unfortunately, it transpired that the days when Damon Hill would challenge for the championship were over after he was dismissed by Williams and his seat given to Heinz-Harald Frentzen. Hill changed to the Arrows team for 1997 and then to the Jordan team the year after.

Meanwhile, a famous brother had taken over the lead seat at Jordan; Ralf Schumacher.

It was left to Jacques Villeneuve to fight off the challenge of Schumacher and the born-again Ferrari 310B. Villeneuve drove a superb season in taking seven victories against Michael Schumacher's five.

Yet, they were pipped at the post by David Coulthard in the first outing in Australia, after Eddie Irvine had sent Villeneuve out of the race. Coulthard took his second victory that year, in Italy.

The greatest excitement (apart from Hill almost winning in Hungary and Ralf Schumacher nudging his brother out of the race in Luxembourg) came in the final race, in the European Grand Prix at Jerez. There was just one point between Villeneuve and Schumacher and Schumacher was leading on lap 48. Like Ayrton Senna before him, Schumacher was a fearless, and therefore on occasion, reckless, driver. On lap 48 Villeneuve spotted a gap and dived inside of Schumacher. Now slightly behind Villeneuve, Schumacher tried to stop him from overtaking and struck the Williams. Fortunately, Schumacher only succeeding in ending the race for his Ferrari, whereas Villeneuve managed to stay on the track and come home in third place. That was all he needed; he had become the world champion.

That almost repetition of the scenario played out between Schumacher and Damon Hill, led to Schumacher being stripped of all his championship points. It meant that Heinz-Harald Frentzen moved into second place and the Williams team were now first and second, with David Coulthard and Jean Alesi in joint third place. Mika Häkkinen was joint fifth with Gerhard Berger in the table at the end of the season.

After that clash between Schumacher and Villeneuve during the last race of the season, Häkkinen took the chequered flag first; with hindsight, it was the Finn throwing down the gauntlet, and those who picked it up in 1998 had a hard time sustaining the challenge.

Villeneuve's Williams faded that year, the year that Ralf Schumacher squeezed into the number ten spot and Damon Hill got a rare look in driving his Jordan-Mugen-Honda, finishing on the number six spot. His Jordan was simply outclassed though he claimed victory in Belgium. The fight now was between Michael Schumacher, and Mika Häkkinen in the McLaren-Mercedes, with David Coulthard and Eddie Irvine battling it out for third and fourth places. Coulthard undertook a supporting role for his teammate, allowing Häkkinen to take victory at Melbourne, for example.

Changes to the rules meant that the cars were now narrower, thus reducing their downforce, and hence the speed as well.

Häkkinen took four of the first six races, winning an impressive eight in total (he didn't start at Imola and suffered a grid failure at Montréal) in comparison to

Schumacher's five. The final race of the season at Suzuka had the unusual spectacle of Schumacher stalling on the grid and starting out last. In an extraordinary drive, he took himself to third place only to be defeated when debris on the track blew out his tire. Nonetheless, Häkkinen's championship was well earned with eleven podium finishes, six fastest laps and nine pole positions in thirteen completed races.

Ferrari must have harboured great hopes, however, for the following year. They were disappointed once more, because Mika Häkkinen completed a dramatic year at the front once more, after scrapping with Irvine, Coulthard and Heinz-Harald Frentzen, who suffered a fractured leg in a crash at Montréal. And suddenly, Rubens Barrichello popped back up in the table for the first time since 1996. Ralf Schumacher had the unusual experience of coming home in sixth position, right behind brother Michael on fifth, thanks to the fact that Schumacher senior had broken his leg in the British Grand Prix (where Häkkinen lost his entire back wheel) and only returned with a metal plate in his leg for the final two races of the season to try and assist Eddie Irvine and his Ferrari, in his teammate's fierce challenge for the title.

Irvine won his first Grand Prix victory in Australia, led the field by 8 points at one stage, and had a 4-point advantage in the final race, by which time he had won three more. But it was not to be; Häkkinen was on superb form and became the seventh man in the history of Formula One to triumph on two successive occasions.

Hopes had also been high for Damon Hill this year, but success did not materialise. True, he came fifth in Britain, but he hadn't enjoyed a good season, and retired from the sport.

One cannot help but feel disappointed that his potential was left unused after his winning World Championship drive.

Mika Häkkinen

ABOVE:
Nigel Mansell (Williams) at the 1991
United States Grand Prix, Phoenix

LEFT:
Nigel Mansell drives the Williams-
Renault FW14 during the Spanish
Grand Prix at the Circuit de Catalunya,
Barcelona, 29th September 1991

Barcelona: Grand Prix of Spain, Michael Schumacher , 15th May 1992

ABOVE:
Aerial view of Ayrton Senna of Brazil in
action in his McLaren Ford during the
Monaco Grand Prix at the Monte Carlo
circuit. Senna finished in first place,
24th May 1993

LEFT:
Ayrton Senna of Brazil in action in his
McLaren Honda during the Monaco
Grand Prix at the Monte Carlo circuit.
Senna finished in first place, 1992

Ayrton Senna of Brazil is attended to by medics on the track after he crashed into the concrete barrier with his Rothmans Williams car during the early stages of the San Marino Formula One Grand Prix at Imola. Senna sustained serious head injuries in the accident and was airlifted to hospital where he later died, 1st May 1994

Damon Hill in the Williams at his one
and only pitstop during the race,
changing from rain to slick tyres,
Sao Paulo, Brazil, 1996

Monaco Grand Prix, Monte Carlo; Mika Hakkinen of Mercedes Mclaren , 15th May 1999

FERRARI PLAYS HARD TO GET

When the cars lined up for the first race of the new millennium, the fifty-first season of FIA Formula One racing, there was great expectation in the Ferrari camp that this had to be their season. They had reason to be optimistic; the Ferrari and McLaren—Mercedes teams had dominated the championship, the previous year, excluding every other car from the winner's podium with the exception of Damon Hill and Heinz-Harald Frentzen's two wins in the Jordan-Mugen-Honda and Johnny Herbert in the Stewart-Ford. Rubens Barrichello must not have believed his good fortune when he was asked to replace Eddie Irvine in the second Ferrari seat.

The Williams team now joined up with BMW for their engines, whereas the BAR team had turned to Honda for their magic. The Stewart team, meanwhile, had been renamed and now started as Jaguar Racing, with Eddie Irvine as the driver. And, especially for British fans, there was a new face on the grid space and, indeed, on the table at the end of the season; it was Jenson Button, who sat behind the wheel of the Williams—BMW and made a creditable start, coming home eighth with 12 points.

From the off, Schumacher showed that he intended to take the title this season, by winning the opening three Grands Prix, and after race ten, in Austria, despite Mika Häkkinen's win, he was leading the table with 56 points to Coulthard's 50. Roles were reversed after the Hungarian, the twelfth Grand Prix, in which Häkkinen drove a magnificent race to top the table on 64 points to Schumacher's 62. Coulthard was third with 58, but there was very little in it and all to play for. In Belgium, Schumacher forced Häkkinen onto the grass at 200 miles an hour (321 km/h); that incident could have spelt more than disaster, but the Finn recovered, drove superbly and took the race.

Italy, then, was the start of Schumacher's comeback. Frentzen caused a three-car spin with Barrichello and Jarno Trulli, and Coulthard become involved in the melée. None of the teams realised at the time that fire marshal Paolo Ghislimberti had been killed when a wheel from this accident struck him on the chest. Schumacher won the restarted competition; he later broke into tears at the news, firstly that the marshal had been killed and secondly that he now had

forty-one wins and had equalled Ayrton Senna's record. The final two races went Schumacher's way when Häkkinen was forced to retire and then was penalised for jumping the start. Ferrari had their first championship in twenty-one years, and Schumacher was on the road to motor racing superstardom. 108 points was an impressive record.

Another piece of heart-warming news that year was that Stirling Moss, already an OBE, was awarded a knighthood.

For the next four years there was only one winning combination; Ferrari and Michael Schumacher. It was a truly remarkable success story. There were other stories, too, of course; those years contained the gradual ascent of another Finn, Kimi-Matias Räikkönen, whose fresh face appeared in 2001 in what turned out to be Häkkinen's final shot at the title. But Mika was out of luck, and perhaps it was the memory of a tepid season when he gained only 37 points that finally swayed him to jettison his helmet. Juan Pablo Montoya from Colombia made his debut this year and could be well pleased with his sixth place, and for the next few years he would prove a force to be reckoned with that others ignored at their peril. 2001 was the year that David Coulthard might have won the championship had he been driving against anyone else but Michael Schumacher in full flood. Coulthard came second, the closest he had come or would ever come again. Ralf Schumacher finished the season fourth in his Williams-BMW and would finish the next season in the same position, which was as high as he would ever be placed on the table. It wasn't easy being the brother of a superstar, yet he did very well this season taking three victories from his brother, leaving just two apiece for Coulthard and Häkkinen.

In 2001, Schumacher lapped up another nine wins and 123 points. Yet in 2002, he even topped this by finishing either first or second in every race except in Malaysia, and even there he finished third, so that he had stood on the podium for every race that season, an astonishing achievement.

Benetton had been sold to Renault, now back in F1 racing, and Toyota had joined the fray, whereas the Prost GP team had been liquidated. It was a bad year for the Arrows team, too, as financial problems caused them to implode

after the German Grand Prix. Their driver, Heinz-Harald Frentzen, had left the team shortly before, which meant frustration for him as he could no longer compete that season. But Rubens Barrichello, partnering Michael Schumacher in a Ferrari, improved on his surge upwards, begun in the previous seasons, as, indeed, did Juan Pablo Montoya in the Williams-BMW; they were rewarded with second and third placings respectively. Jenson Button got a second peek at the table in his Renault, coming seventh. Button would have to be patient and wait a few years for his turn to reach the summit.

Controversy never seemed to be far from Michael Schumacher and in Austria he was handed the victory by Barrichello, who allowed him to pass on the final lap. At the podium ceremony the crowd jeered, angered that the spirit of racing been tarnished and Schumacher's standing dropped considerably. Barrichello, Schumacher and Ferrari were slapped with a fine of one million US Dollars, but there were no rules in force as yet against such actions on the track; the fine was imposed for the failure to observe Article 170 of the Formula One Sporting Regulations regarding the podium ceremony, when Schumacher and Barrichello had swapped trophies and Schumacher drew Barrichello onto the winner's podium. The FIA soon introduced new rules to prohibit the artificial alteration of race results.

The Ferrari-Schumacher bandwagon rolled on through into 2003, although it was a much closer-fought contest, which marked the rise of Kimi Räikkönen in a McLaren-Mercedes MP4-17 as a fierce rival for the title; just two points separated them in the season, 93 to 91, even though Räikkönen only won in Malaysia. It was the Finn's first Grand Prix victory, but it would not be the last. And there was Juan Pablo Montoya, again, tenaciously snapping at their heels. Schumacher's win this year meant that he had beaten Fangio's record, which had stood for forty-six years.

Michael Schumacher

The year had its fair share of drama; monsoon conditions swept the circuit in Brazil, where Mark Webber's Jaguar crashed and Fernando Alonso sent tyres bouncing onto the track after he hit a barrier. Fernando Alonso was in the news again that year when he became the youngest-ever winner of a Grand Prix race, aged 22 years and 26 days, after he won the Hungarian Grand Prix, thus breaking Bruce McLaren's record. *"A dream come true"*, as he described it.

Giancarlo Fisichella secured his first F1 win since entering Formula One in 1996, in his Jordan-Ford, one of only three career victories for the Italian. The race was abandoned with 15 laps left to go, but Fisichella was denied the joy of the podium because the prize was only awarded one week later.

On a lighter, though no less dangerous, note, the priest Cornelius **"Neil"** Horan ran onto the track heading towards the oncoming cars, wearing a green kilt and waving religious banners. Several cars had to swerve to avoid him and he was later jailed. Motor racing produces extremes of all kinds it seems. Behind the scenes, the changes this year included the introduction of the HANS device. Made of carbon fibre in a U shape and sitting in the nape of the neck, it was intended to reduce head injuries, and despite complaints from many drivers, became mandatory in 2003.

The FIA also made an attempt to help the less financially secure teams by introducing one-lap qualifying as a way for smaller teams to receive more television exposure. Something even more important had changed, too. To try and prevent runaway winners taking the sting out of the competition, as Schumacher had the year before, the points scoring system was altered so that now, the first eight finishers would be rewarded with 10, 8, 6, 5, 4, 3, 2, 1 points respectively. And Schumacher duly claimed his eighth title finishing in eighth place in Japan.

There were no such problems in 2004 for Schumacher's fifth consecutive championship, his seventh overall, when Ferrari took first and second place. Schumacher had 148 points followed by Barrichello with 140, and Jenson Button having his best year yet with 85

Fernando Alonso

in the BAR-Honda finishing the season third, by which time he had ten podium finishes and one pole to his credit. The German Grand Prix might have been his had he not needed a replacement engine; that violated a new rule, and so he dropped ten places on the grid. But he still came in second, showing the BAR-Honda's exhaust to Alonso; an astonishing achievement

The Schumacher-Ferrari duo were still unstoppable, winning twelve of the first thirteen races, only Jarno Trulli at Monaco putting a stop to his run of victories after five, when Schumacher equalled Nigel Mansell's record set in 1992. That fifth win was his seventy-fifth Grand Prix victory, an impressive feat. Schumacher was denied a chance at beating the record when an incident in the tunnel at Monaco between him and Juan-Pablo Montoya ended the race for the Ferrari driver; as a collision with Ralf Schumacher had done for Alonso earlier.

Brother Michael won the championship in Belgium in August, the fourteenth race of the season, by coming second to Kimi Räikkönen, after Webber had caused a pile up at the start that damaged several cars taking out four of them altogether. Apart from that sole win, you had to commiserate with poor Räikkönen; he had to endure a season that saw constant engine failures, so hopes of challenging Schumacher this year were severely dashed.

2004 was the end of the road for Jaguar Racing and Ford. Both withdrew from Formula One.

And suddenly… it was all over.

It was as though the magician had unexpectedly fallen asleep. What had happened? It was 2005. Ferrari's years-long dominance was a nightmare relegated to the past. A new era had dawned without anyone realising it. The dam had been breached and the water came flooding in.

Nineteen races were waiting.

There was a new bull in the pit; literally. Jaguar had been bought by Red Bull and became Red Bull Racing. Red Bull even acquired it's own circuit in 2011 in Austria, The Red Bull Ring, which had once been the Österreichring.

Some rules changed; a restart would now take place behind the safety car instead of from a standing start, after a race had been red-flagged. Neither would the timekeeping system stop; engines were required to endure two Grands Prix without being changed.

There was another rule change that seemed to prove fatal to Ferrari, instrumental, perhaps, in their astonishing collapse. Tyre changes were prohibited during the course of a race. Ferrari used Bridgestone tyres, and their performance/reliability equation was knocked off kilter for the season. Badly. Those cars driving on Michelin tyres went on to glory.

So who were they?

Spain's pride and joy, Fernando Alonso and Renault were the season's new dream team. Alonso had been in F1 since 2001. Then there was Kimi Räikkönen and his McLaren-Mercedes and then… well, way back in the distance you might have seen a Ferrari somewhere with a disgruntled Michael Schumacher at the wheel, who came forward for one victory in the US.

But the season belonged to the persistent Alonso.

The Renault was in blistering form this year and Alonso took seven victories hauling in the title with a second place in Brazil and two Grands Prix still to go. It was a momentous occasion for the Spaniard for another reason; he had won the title as the youngest-ever champion, trumping Emerson Fittipaldi; he was 24 years and 59 days old at the time. Alonso remains the only Spanish driver to have won a Formula One Grand Prix.

Kimi Räikkönen was a fierce and dangerous challenger but was dogged by engine problems yet again; three failures practically ruined his chances.

And Jenson Button had even worse luck. He was in dispute over his contract with Williams, by opting to remain with BAR-Honda, suffered a crash, had a third place written off because of a technical infringement, and had a two-race ban imposed on his BAR-Honda team when San Marino inspectors discovered a hidden fuel compartment enabling the cars to run below weight. The temptation to cheat for the glory of the podium had often proved irresistible, even if immoral. Button soldiered on for ninth place.

Alonso had no intention of yielding to Schumacher again, and as it turned out, he didn't. After a bad year in 2005, third after Räikkönen and far behind Alonso, everyone waited with baited breath for Schumacher to come steamrolling back in 2006, and it wasn't for lack of trying that the championship eluded him. Alonso and he fought like tigers all the way, providing an enthralling battle for supremacy. The tug of war moved in Alonso's favour in the early races, swinging over to Schumacher before returning to Alonso for a string of four back-to-back victories that gave him six wins and three second places from the first nine races. The tussle intensified as Schumacher went all out, and Alonso didn't win again until the penultimate race in Japan, whilst the German driver won five. Both had suffered engine trouble that had put them out of races, Schumacher's woes coming at the penultimate and crucial Japanese Grand Prix. It was divine justice by the gods of the circuit, however.

Aficionados delight in the final race being a championship decider, and this year gave them one, although neither of the main contenders won at Brazil. Felipe Massa did, the first Brazilian since Ayrton Senna to do so, and secured his second 2006 Grand Prix of eleven career victories.

Schumacher fought through from tenth to fourth at Brazil but it was not enough. Alonso took second place. At the British Grand Prix Alonso had become the youngest-ever driver to achieve a triple, pole, fastest lap and race, and now he had become the youngest driver to take a double championship, winning this year with 134 points to Schumacher's 121. Alonso had been resoundingly triumphant for two seasons, a heady achievement for the Spaniard.

By this time, everyone sensed that an era of extraordinary triumphs had ended for one driver. Perhaps he, too, had realised that his moment had passed; a driver's shelf life is inevitably limited and this driver was now 37 years old. But he had determinedly and magnificently taken his chances with both hands firmly on the wheel. The thunderclap announcement had come in Italy. Michael Schumacher, the most successful driver in the history of the Grand Prix had called it a day.

On a lesser note, for the first time since 1956, there had been not one British constructor represented on the winner's podiums, though there was British pride when David Coulthard reached his 200th Grand Prix in Barcelona and so became a member of the prestigious '200 Club'. And Nick Heidfeld, driving for Sauber-BMW, squeezed his nose into the top ten for only the second time, the first time was 2002, coming in ninth place with 23 points, ahead of Ralf Schumacher on 20. Heidfeld's debut Grand Prix had been in the year 2000 and his third top-ten placing would come in the 2007 season when he would finish fifth.

But if 2006 had seen the farewell of one champion, 2007 saw the birth of another. There was a 'new kid on the grid', and a kid with the attitude that Schumacher would have approved of. His name was Lewis Hamilton and he debuted that year in the McLaren-Mercedes teaming up with Fernando Alonso.

And it was quite an extraordinary and exciting first season for the young British driver not to mention British fans. Hamilton was up front from the word go, battling for the honours as part of a trio of front runners with Fernando Alonso and Kimi Räikkönen, in one of the most closely contested fights for the title that Formula One had ever seen. Hamilton's debut was even more impressive than Michael Schumacher's had been, and he came third in the season's first outing. His first winner's podium was not long in coming, and it arrived at the sixth race, in Canada, which he followed up immediately with another win in the United States, one of four that season, as the Ferraris and McLarens thrashed out the placings between them.

Another Finnish driver was making a good F1 debut that season; Heikki Kovalainen, who eventually finished seventh in his Renault.

It was a season of drama; Hamilton suffered an almighty crash during qualifying in Germany and started tenth on the grid. During a torrential downpour, the car aquaplaned and skidded off the track on lap 4; Hungary produced a 'controversial incident' between the two McLaren drivers, which resulted in Alonso being demoted to sixth on the grid. In Canada, there were four safety car starts, and during treacherous weather in Japan, Hamilton spun off the track again. It was to be another of those final race deciders, this time in Brazil, and Hamilton was leading the pack with 107 points.

The championship, then, was Hamilton's for the taking, but cruel fate determined that he would be defeated by a gearbox problem, which set him back from second to seventh place when crossing the line; that put him joint second with Alonso on 109 points, just one point behind Räikkönen. Räikkönen had taken his first title, the third of his countrymen to drive to glory. It was a bittersweet ending to an incredible season for the young British driver, who had landed nine consecutive podium finishes and set up a record for a F1 newcomer.

For 2007, it was compulsory for both compounds of tyre to be used at least once during the race. The softs were painted with a white stripe, and all cars were fitted with red, blue and yellow LED cockpit lights so that drivers would know about track signals or conditions on the circuit.

Hamilton brought more drama with him into the 2008 season, although this time, his new rival was Felipe Massa in the Ferrari, and again, it was a mighty wrestling match that would be decided by one point in the last race. A double-edged sword for British fans' nerves.

Standardised engine control units (ECUs) were compulsory in 2008, so no more traction control, and gearboxes had to last for four races.

Hamilton set down the markers in the very first race in Australia, but the next four victories see-sawed between Massa and Räikkönen. Throughout the season, mercifully devoid of too many dangerous incidents, Hamilton and Massa drew ahead until there was just the final race to filter out the winner.

Needing only fifth place to win, Hamilton kept his team and country on tenterhooks until the final bend of the final lap when he overtook Timo Glock of Toyota and claimed his reward; the World Championship. He was the youngest ever champion and the ninth British holder of the coveted prize. Truly an astonishing year for him.

Hamilton was just starting out, but another British driver, the Scot David Coulthard, decided that his time behind the wheel was now over and it was time to move on to other things. On 25 November 2008, he took over a chair at the BBC to become a commentator for Formula One races on TV.

Although Hamilton was out of luck in 2009, British fans weren't, because this was the year when Jenson Button would shine in his Brawn-Mercedes. His shadow was going to be the German driver Sebastian Vettel in an RBR-Renault; Vettel had started driving in F1 in 2007, winning for the first time in Italy the year after and was about to take the motor racing world by storm in a way that was reminiscent of the Michael Schumacher juggernaut.

Many changes had been introduced to try and get a more wheel-to-wheel competitive edge into the races; one of these was the reintroduction of slick tyres, to decrease driver reliance on aerodynamic downforce; wet tyres were now renamed 'intermediates'; extreme weather

Jenson Button

95

tyres were now just 'wet' tyres. Front wings were lower and wider, with the rear wings higher and narrower. Finally, to improve the downforce and aid overtaking, adjustable front wings were permitted.

So, armed with eight engines to last the season, the teams launched into a struggle between Button in the Brawn-Mercedes and Vettel in the Red Bull-Renault. Of the two Brits out there, it was crystal clear who was determined to grab the limelight this time. Jenson Button took the first race in Australia, and so Button and Brawn-Mercedes became the first team to start on pole and win the race on their debut since Mercedes-Benz in 1954. A double of sorts for Mercedes.

After a messy start in which Button got clean away, the British driver soon opened up a four second lead, with Vettel in pursuit and Hamilton working his way up from eighteenth position to ninth. Button took his pit stop on lap 19 and came out ahead, driving well and in no danger. It was Vettel who hit a wall and damaged his wheel towards the end, and with debris on the track, this led to only the second safety car finish in Formula One racing. Button had secured his first spectacular win and delivered his warning. If you can't beat me, you're not in with a chance.

Vettel took up the challenge but couldn't get to the line first until the third race, after which he saw nothing but Button's tail for the next four outings. At twenty-nine years of age and a decade in major league motor racing, Button eventually finished with 95 points to Vettel's 84, and took the crown, Britain's tenth World Champion. Proof that with the right hardware, a good driver can always excel.

New kid on the grid this year was Bruno Senna, the nephew of racing legend Ayrton Senna. But history would not repeat itself in the same family as far as talent was concerned, and after the 2012 season, during which he completed the fastest lap in Belgium, Senna's F1 career was over when Williams dropped him.

2010 turned out to be a cracking year, although the two British drivers were shown the back seat by a dynamic Vettel and an Alonso resurgence. Not for want of trying did they only manage fourth and fifth places; Button hit the winner's podium

Sebastian Vettel

twice and Hamilton three times. In fact, the top place was wrenched back and forth between drivers no less than nine times over the course of the season. Until midway through, it was uncertain whether Red Bull, Mercedes or Renault would be ultimately victorious. Mark Webber, Vettel's partner, was having a great season in his Renault, too, and took four victories. Webber had been in F1 since 2002 and scored his first victory in 2009, one of eight podiums.

Resentment in a second driver often bubbles to the surface if they feel they are being given less attention, and this year, the problem surfaced between Vettel and Webber and also Alonso and Massa. As the season drew to a close and the inter-team rivalry became verbal, Red Bull insisted that its drivers were free of team orders and could do as they wished, whereas Alonso was favoured without a second thought by Ferrari. This benefitted the Spaniard, because with just two races left to go, he topped the table eleven points clear of Webber, with Massa having fallen a long way down. By the last race in Abu Dhabi, the title was up for grabs by three drivers; Vettel, Alonso and Webber. Hamilton would have needed divine intervention to join them.

Just for the record, it wasn't forthcoming.

Vettel had to come ahead of Alonso by sixteen points to take the title; it was a Herculean task, but when the unfortunate Spaniard got stuck in midfield, Vettel took off and was only seen by his rivals again after the flag. It had been a record season for the young German. Young he was; in fact, he had now assumed the title of the youngest World Champion, at the age of 23 years and 134 days.

Vettel had beaten his fellow German Michael Schumacher that year; Schumacher had decided that he wanted another bite at the cherry and was convinced that he could grab that eighth title. He had overestimated himself, and fourth would be his best position before he called it a day once more; the young drivers were sharper and faster, even though Schumacher was still his old ruthless self and almost shoved Barrichello into a wall.

The Vettel steamroller drove onwards for the next three years, and it seemed as though the German might emulate Schumacher, so untouchable he seemed to be. Everyone hoped that if that was to be the case then at least there would be exciting challenges to look forward to, for no one wanted a repeat of the deadly certainty of those Ferrari years. And indeed, Vettel was looking over his shoulder during those years, first at Button and then at Alonso, with Australian

Mark Webber biting everyone's heels.

But Vettel continued his domination of the table with an impressive 2011 season in which he lost only two of the first eight races, conceding to Lewis Hamilton and then Jenson Button. Only Webber and Alonso were also able to take a race apiece. At Brazil, the final race of the season, Vettel broke Nigel Mansell's record by taking his fifteenth pole position, and he became the youngest driver to take a second championship; 24 years and 98 days old.

For the next two years, it was left up to Alonso to try and unseat the champion, although seven different drivers took one race each in the early part of the 2012 season. Pirelli had now taken over the tyre manufacture for F1, but the rapid degradation of their compounds on the track was causing problems.

Although Alonso eventually took three races in 2012 and Button and Hamilton took three and four apiece, four consecutive wins starting in Singapore brought Vettel back into the running, so that the last race in Brazil would be the decider. It went to Jenson Button, who was too far back in the title race, however, to make a difference at the top.

Many felt that Alonso had been the driver of the season, but he was destined to be runner up when Vettel came in sixth to claim his title for the third consecutive year and as the youngest driver to make that triple.

Pushed out of the table altogether, Michael Schumacher could now see that his moment had passed and he retired again.

Lewis Hamilton had wanted a new challenge and Mercedes welcomed him into their corner to fill the seat Schumacher had vacated.

Footnote to the season; Mexican Sergio Perez squeezed his Sauber-Ferrari onto the table in tenth place this year. Perez had debuted in 2011.

The Vettel steamroller thundered on throughout 2013 giving the driver his most decisive victory to date; 397 points to Alonso's 242. Vettel won the championship for the fourth consecutive season with four races still to complete, only the third driver in sixty-four years of Formula One to do so. He eventually took thirteen of the nineteen races, with nine consecutive wins to finish the season, a spread to equal Alberto Ascari's record of 1952/53. To the despair of everyone else, he seemed as unassailable in his Red Bull-Renault as Schumacher had been in his Ferrari. But the tensions between Webber and Vettel boiled over when Vettel ignored the team's instructions to Webber's detriment. Upset at what he considered to be the preferential treatment afforded to Vettel, Webber left F1 racing at the end of the season.

F1 now bid farewell to the 2.4-litre V8 engine configuration that had been used since 2006. For the new season of 2014, a 1.6-litre turbocharged V6 engine formula would be used. It was hello to Russia for the first time in a century when the sixteenth race of the season was held at Sochi. New rules meant that engines had to last for at least 2,500 miles (4,000 km) before being changed and the minimum weight of cars was now 1,415 lbs (642 kg) to 1,523 lbs (691 kg). Scarily, there would now be double points for the final race of the season.

What would 2014 bring? Everyone knew what to expect.

What no one expected was to see Vettel humbled; and yet that was the scenario. It was one of the most extraordinary upsets in F1 history, with Vettel squeezed off the winners' podiums completely, and the man who did the squeezing was former champion Lewis Hamilton.

Both he and Vettel were forced to retire in the first race, so no one was any the wiser about what was going happen. But from Malaysia on, beginning with four consecutive wins, Hamilton stormed to a magnificent eleven victories, holding off repeated challenges by his teammate Nico Rosberg to do so. Mercedes took all except three victories, because Rosberg took five races and came second that year. 384 points saw Hamilton take his second championship with Rosberg second on 317, and way above Vettel in fifth place with 167.

There had been two, almost new kids on the grids this year; Daniel Ricciardo had climbed into Webber's old seat for Red Bull and kept the team's flag flying by driving a terrific season and finishing in third place. Finnish driver Valtteri Bottas had a great season too, coming fourth with Williams.

One accident left the 2014 F1 season with a tragedy, the first fatal accident since 1994. Frenchman Jules Bianchi lost control of his Anglo-Russian Marussia in extremely wet conditions, and he collided with a recovery vehicle, during the Japanese Grand Prix. He went into a coma from which he never recovered and died on 17 July 2015 after spending nine months in a coma following the accident. It was a terrible and painful reminder of what danger the F1 driver finds himself in for the duration of every race.

So with the tables turned, in 2015 Hamilton was the boy to beat and he proved a hard nut to crack, leading the table ahead of Rosberg and Vettel, in a season that was primarily a supreme battle between these three superb drivers. Valtteri Bottas made his presence felt and Kimi Räikkönen and Philipe

Massa proved that they are also first class drivers, as did the Russian Daniil Vyacheslavovich Kvyat — who first raced in Formula One in 2014 and now partners Daniel Ricciardo. These were the drivers who eventually filled the first seven places on the table. After a great season, Kyvat was just able to hold off his teammate and finish on seventh place.

Vettel was within three points of the lead at one stage in the season, and one of the most remarkable races took place when the teams lined up in the United States on the 25th October; Hamilton was 66 points clear of Vettel on the table. The track was wet, there was a collision involving Massa and Alonso on the first lap, and only twelve cars were destined to reach the finish line. Hamilton and Ricciardo battled for the lead until Rosberg managed to get in front on lap 18; he was still there on lap 27. Another collision on lap 36 then took out Ricciardo and Hülkenberg. On lap 43 it was Daniil Kvyat's turn to have an accident.

All efforts by the other leading drivers were in ultimately in vain, however, after Rosberg lost the lead to Hamilton on lap 48 when his rear wheels started to spin causing him to slide off the track.

Lewis Hamilton had taken control of the racetracks for the third consecutive year and after eleven pole positions, he claimed his third World Championship by winning the USA leg of the competition with three races still to go, decisive proof that Hamilton is one of the top driver's of all time. Hamilton eventually took 381 points to Rosberg's 322 with Rosberg winning the final three races of the season.

The competition is as fierce and ruthless as it has ever been, and the champions at the top of Formula One racing such as Lewis Hamilton, Michael Schumacher or Ayrton Senna, arrived there as the result of breathtaking skill, fervent passion, ice-cool nerves, and the top-class teamwork that Formula One motor racing demands.

Truly a sport whose revered heroes are blessed with incomparable fearlessness, it is also an unpredictable progression of incomparable thrills, heartrending tragedies, many tears, and magnificent triumphs.

Lewis Hamilton

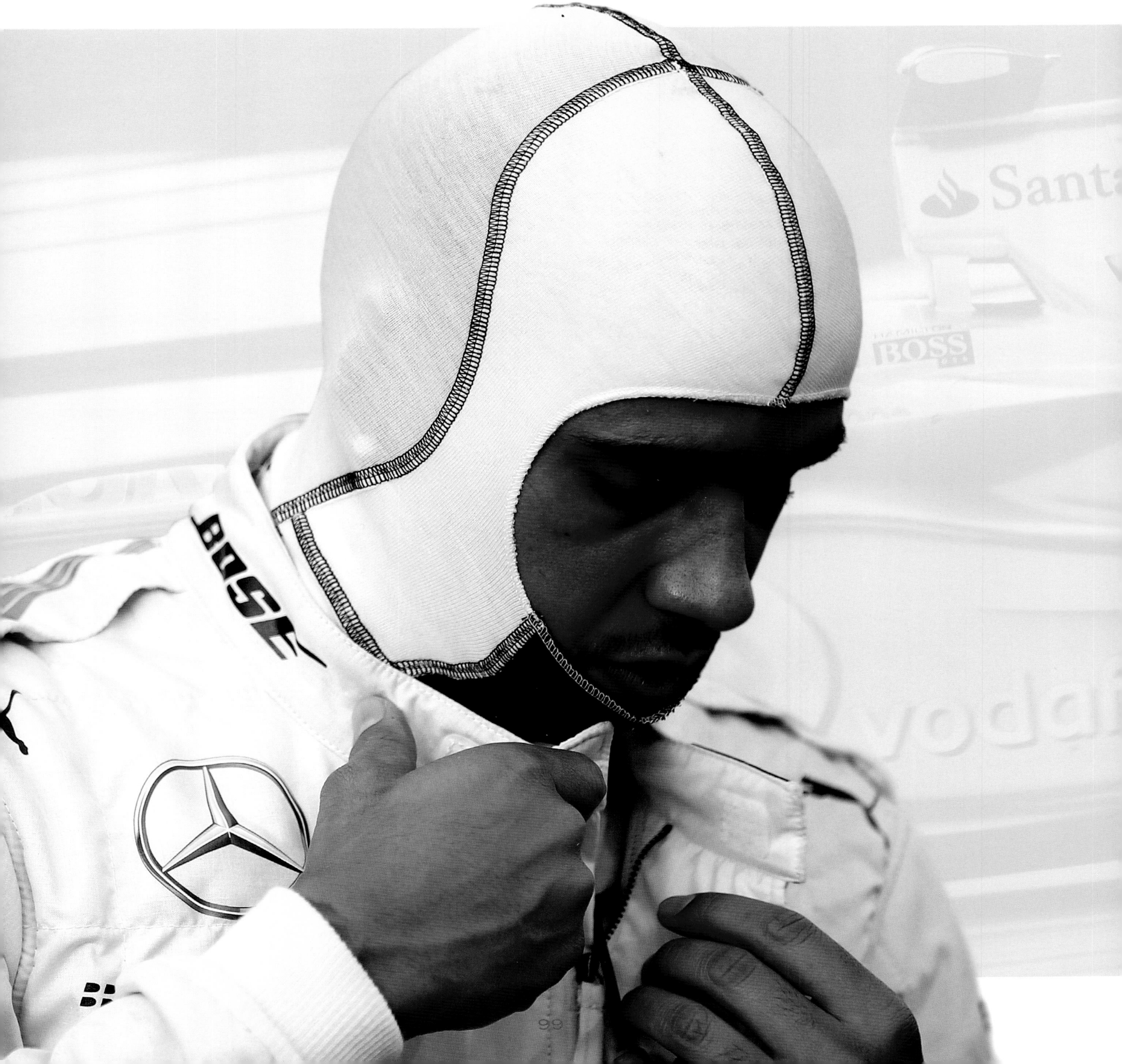
BOSS

Take me for a ride, rain master!, Europe Grand Prix, Nuerburgring, 21 May 2000

ABOVE:
Spanish Renault driver Fernando
Alonso (R) celebrates on the podium
next to German Ferrari driver Michael
Schumacher (L) after winning the
Bahrain Formula One Grand Prix at
Sakhir racetrack in Manama,
12th March 2006

LEFT:
Michael Schumacher driving for Ferrari
at the 2006 Canadian Grand Prix

Fernando Alonso of Spain and Renault holds off the challenge of Michael Schumacher of Germany and Ferrari during the Bahrain Formula One Grand Prix at the Bahrain International Circuit in Sakhir, 12th March 2006

ABOVE:
Sebastian Vettel of Germany and Red Bull Racing looks on from his cockpit during Formula One winter testing at the Ricardo Tormo circuit in Valencia, Spain, 26th February 2009

RIGHT:
Sebatian Vettel of Germany celebrates winning the Formula One Indian Grand Prix 2013 at the Buddh International circuit in Greater Noida, on the outskirts of New Delhi, 27th October 2013

Max Verstappen of Netherlands attends a seat fitting ahead of the Japanese Formula One Grand Prix at Suzuka Circuit in Suzuka, 2nd October 2014

Lewis Hamilton of Great Britain and Mercedes GP celebrates with the team in the pit lane after winning the United States Formula One Grand Prix and the championship at Circuit of The Americas in Austin, 25th October 2015

DRIVER'S CHAMPIONSHIP WINNERS BY SEASON

SEASON	DRIVER	TEAM	WINS	POINTS	SEASON	DRIVER	TEAM	WINS	POINTS
1950	Guiseppe Farina	Alfa Romeo	3	30	1984	Niki Lauda	McLaren	5	72
1951	Juan Manuel Fangio	Alfa Romeo	3	31	1985	Alain Prost	McLaren	5	73
1952	Alberto Ascari	Ferrari	6	36	1986	Alain Prost	McLaren	4	72
1953	Alberto Ascari	Ferrari	5	34.5	1987	Nelson Piquet	Williams	3	73
1954	Juan Manuel Fangio	Maserati / Mercedes	6	42	1988	Ayrton Senna	McLaren	8	90
1955	Juan Manuel Fangio	Mercedes	4	40	1989	Alain Prost	McLaren	4	76
1956	Juan Manuel Fangio	Ferrari	3	30	1990	Ayrton Senna	McLaren	6	78
1957	Juan Manuel Fangio	Maserati	4	40	1991	Ayrton Senna	McLaren	7	96
1958	Mike Hawthorne	Ferrari	1	42	1992	Nigel Mansell	Williams	9	108
1959	Jack Brabham	Cooper	2	31	1993	Alain Prost	Williams	7	99
1960	Jack Brabham	Cooper	5	43	1994	Michael Schumacher	Benetton	8	92
1961	Phil Hill	Ferrari	2	34	1995	Michael Schumacher	Benetton	9	102
1962	Graham Hill	BRM	4	42	1996	Damon Hill	Williams	8	97
1963	Jim Clark	Lotus	7	54	1997	Jacques Villeneuve	Williams	7	81
1964	John Surtees	Ferrari	2	40	1998	Mika Häkkinen	McLaren	8	100
1965	Jim Clark	Lotus	6	54	1999	Mika Häkkinen	McLaren	5	76
1966	Jack Brabham	Brabham	4	42	2000	Michael Schumacher	Ferrari	9	108
1967	Denny Hulme	Brabham	2	51	2001	Michael Schumacher	Ferrari	9	123
1968	Graham Hill	Lotus	3	48	2002	Michael Schumacher	Ferrari	11	144
1969	Jackie Stewart	Matra	6	63	2003	Michael Schumacher	Ferrari	6	93
1970	Jochen Rindt	Lotus	5	45	2004	Michael Schumacher	Ferrari	13	148
1971	Jackie Stewart	Tyrell	6	62	2005	Fernando Alonso	Renault	7	133
1972	Emerson Fittipaldi	Lotus	5	61	2006	Fernando Alonso	Renault	7	134
1973	Jackie Stewart	Tyrell	5	71	2007	Kimi Räikkönen	Ferrari	6	110
1974	Emerson Fittipaldi	McLaren	3	55	2008	Lewis Hamilton	McLaren	5	98
1975	Niki Lauda	Ferrari	5	64.5	2009	Jenson Button	Brawn	6	95
1976	James Hunt	McLaren	6	69	2010	Sebastian Vettel	Red Bull	5	256
1977	Niki Lauda	Ferrari	3	72	2011	Sebastian Vettel	Red Bull	11	392
1978	Mario Andretti	Lotus	6	64	2012	Sebastian Vettel	Red Bull	5	281
1979	Jody Scheckter	Ferrari	3	51	2013	Sebastian Vettel	Red Bull	13	397
1980	Alan Jones	Williams	5	67	2014	Lewis Hamilton	Mercedes	11	384
1981	Nelson Piquet	Brabham	3	50	2015	Lewis Hamilton	Mercedes	10	381
1982	Keke Rosberg	Williams	1	44	2016	Nico Rosberg	Mercedes	9	385
1983	Nelson Piquet	Brabham	3	59	2017	Lewis Hamilton	Mercedes	9	363